South-East Asia

1930–1970

D. Kummer
1993

.50

South-East Asia
1930–1970

THE LEGACY OF COLONIALISM
AND NATIONALISM

Fred R. von der Mehden

W · W · NORTON & COMPANY · INC · New York

To Louise Whitehead, who loves books

First American edition 1974

Library of Congress Cataloging in Publication Data

von der Mehden, Fred R.
  South-East Asia, 1930–1970.

  (Library of world civilization series)
  Bibliography:

1. Asia, Southeastern – History. 2. Asia,
Southeastern – Politics. I. Title.
DS518.1.V66   1974   959   73–14767

ISBN 0-393-05513-2
ISBN 0-393-09320-4   (pbk.)

Printed and bound in Great Britain by Jarrold and Sons Ltd, Norwich

Contents

Preface

Any perceptive foreign observer who has worked in South-East Asia during the post-war decades has seen both the influence of the past and the monumental changes that have made their imprint on the region. It is not our intention to present chronologically oriented contemporary history. Throughout we shall attempt to be comparative and analytical, although personal impressions will be noted. The first three chapters set out to review the forces present in the latter years of the colonial period and the changes wrought by the Japanese occupation during the Second World War and by the early post-war nationalist struggles. In the process, we shall stress the impact of the developments of this period on future events, attitudes and institutions. The next three chapters look back upon the post-war years from the vantage point of the 1970s, analysing what happened to the legacies left by the colonial and nationalist eras on ideologies, institutions and society.

A note on place-names: when discussing the pre-independence period we shall use colonial place-names such as the Dutch or Netherlands East Indies and French Indo-China. Contemporary names will be used in describing post-war states, although the term 'Indo-China' will be employed to include Laos, Cambodia and Vietnam. Malaysia is a special case. The name Malaya will be used before 1963, when Malaysia was formed.

My thanks to students and colleagues at Rice University with whom I have discussed some of the ideas expressed herein, and most particularly to Professor John Ambler who has listened and commented on the manuscript over many cups of coffee. Special acknowledgment goes to Jaquie Ehlers for her typing and interpretation of my writing. Appreciation as always to my wife Audrey for her proof-reading and commentary.

1 The Setting

South-East Asia in the inter-war period was thought of more in terms of exotic travel pictures than in those of war and political strife. The Dutch East Indies brought to mind lightly clad Balinese girls or the Johnsons' treks through the jungles of Borneo. Bangkok, Rangoon, Manila, Mandalay and Saigon were far-off cities which even the most intrepid globe-trotter put on his itinerary with some apprehension. Places such as the capitals of Laos, Malaysia and Cambodia were almost unknown. Only the respective mother countries seemed cognizant of the political and economic turmoil that had developed throughout the region in the inter-war decades, and even there those events received short shrift in the metropolitan daily newspapers.

What was South-East Asia like in the third and fourth decades of this century? This chapter will attempt to establish in broad strokes the political, social and economic benchmarks from which we can gauge the changes that have evolved and erupted in the region in the ensuing years. We should begin, however, by noting that the term 'South-East Asia' covers a highly varied set of cultures and should be regarded only as a convenient geographic expression incorporating dissimilar geographic, historical, cultural, economic and political units which became even more separated from one another than previously as a result of the expanding colonial empires.

Geographically, it is even difficult for most outside observers to envisage the very size of the states. 'Tiny Laos' is approximately the size of the United Kingdom, medium-sized countries such as Burma and Thailand are comparable in area to Spain or France, while Indonesia from east to west would stretch fully across the continental United States. Linguistically the area includes half a dozen major national languages and literally hundreds of dialects varying in syntax, tone, vocabulary and script. In religion, almost every major faith has found at least a temporary home. Islam dominates Indonesia and, to a lesser extent, Malaysia; Buddhism is

7

1 The exotic East: nineteenth-century British representation of (left) two Dyaks from Borneo and (right) a priest and a married couple from Java.

the primary faith of Burma, Thailand, Laos, Cambodia and Vietnam; Christianity holds sway in the Philippines; and even Hinduism still persists in Bali and among Indian emigrants to the region. All of these world faiths rest on a substratum of local animistic customs and beliefs. Historically, kingdoms and principalities have warred with one another over the centuries, and the contemporary international politics of South-East Asia cannot be fully understood without noting pre-colonial antipathies between Burmese and Thai, Cambodian and Vietnamese, Vietnamese and Chinese. The expanding empires of Vietnam and Burma were preying on their

neighbours as late as the nineteenth century. Finally, superimposed upon this polyglot region were the European colonial empires, first the Spanish and Portuguese and later the successful domination of the Indies by the Dutch, of Burma and Malaya by the British, of Indo-China by the French and, very late in the game, of the Philippines by the United States. Only Thailand remained independent, as much owing to the jealousies of the European powers as to the resourcefulness of its rulers. Thus the heterogeneous nature of the region, provided we guard against generalization, allows us to compare a notable range of variables within a single area.

2 A European contemplates the statue of the Buddha in the Great Dagon Pagoda, Rangoon, 1826. Religion was to become an important focus for nationalist feeling.

In order not to be overwhelmed by the varied nature of our subject it would appear useful to survey the changes that overtook the people of the region in three stages: the traditional society, the impact of the West on that society, and the nationalist reaction. In surveying the traditional social-political patterns we must always be aware of the considerable local variations that existed among societies which differed in size, leadership roles, types of agricultural practice, social controls, religious values, etc. It is also important to bear in mind that traditional village society has been romanticized both by Western writers and by South-East Asian political leaders who have seen in it either a sharp contrast to today's complex environment or an ideological base for post-independence political actions. Thus it has been pictured as a Utopia plagued by few of the problems of contemporary society, such as pollution or crime, yet maintaining a democratic decision-making apparatus which had brought to bear the participation of all the people. As the late President Sukarno of Indonesia once commented, Indonesian democracy ruled 'when wild and savage tribes still roamed over Europe' and this early experience of democracy was a guide to post-war progress.

Allowing for variations within the region, traditional society in South-East Asia was actually less idyllic than its supporters have made it out to be, and less Hobbesian than the revisionists have claimed. Village life itself tended to be parochial and relatively stable, enjoying little regular contact with the outside. Even as late as the mid-1960s district officers in north-east Thailand reported that they were unable to reach half of their villages even with a four-wheel-drive vehicle during the rainy season. Thus isolated, the villager became closely tied to the land, the family and local religious customs. Decisions were made within the context of the village, usually by elders acting in conjunction with religious leaders. It was not a democratic society in a Western liberal sense, in that individual rights were subservient to the group and structured, organized political competition was not present. Within this closely knit organism social relations, land patterns and religious values were comparatively stable.

A myth of long standing has been that the traditional ruler tyrannized the villagers from above. No doubt rulers were often arbitrary, capricious and cruel, and made impossible demands on the people under their control. Outside the major towns, however, domination from the centre tended to be intermittent in character, the normal pattern being one of governmental neglect interrupted by emergencies usually related to war. In few parts of South-East Asia had tax policies reached the sophistication of China or Japan, and claims on the resources of villagers far from the centres of power tended to be less than systematic. Loyalties were thus more parochial, centred on the village and the family and to a lesser degree on larger political units. People classified themselves by village, family or clan rather than by nation. With the penetration from the West this changed, but even as late as the 1950s it was reported that more than half the population of Laos did not know they were living in Laos.

At the political apex of the pre-European societies of South-East Asia were the kings or sultans, ruling over a largely feudal structure. These rulers were closely identified in the minds of the people with religious norms which were the foundation of their power. While often arbitrary in his decisions and seemingly possessing unlimited power over his subjects, the traditional ruler was usually bound by religious strictures and limited in the exercise of his power by court intrigue, religious leaders and, perhaps most important of all, the technological backwardness of the culture in

3 Colonialism idealized: a British family strolls among clean, respectful natives against the neat red roofs of Singapore, 1846.

which he operated. This last element greatly diminished his ability to exercise continuous control over his subjects and to weld the isolated villages of his polity into a modern nation.

Into this traditional system came the Europeans. Initially the early European traders made little impact on the vast majority of the people of the region. Based largely in the coastal trading centres and with little desire to rule the hinterlands, the Westerners did not penetrate deeply into the region until after the middle of the nineteenth century. Except in the Philippines, the Straits Settlements and parts of the Indies, they were content to allow the local rulers to govern, and the villages remained isolated from outside influences. The next half-century, however, saw two changes which were effectively to restructure much of South-East Asian society. First the European powers moved to consolidate their control over previously independent parts of the region. Burma finally fell to British conquest in 1886, the whole of Indo-China had come under French

4 Contemporary painting of the taking of Hong Hoa, Annam, 1884. France won control over Indo-China only after protracted fighting and frequent insurrections.

5 Market scene in nineteenth-century colonial Indonesia, where the Dutch presence fostered the emergence of a prosperous Chinese business class.

domination by the turn of the century, and in the next decade the Dutch ended the last vestiges of real local independence in the Indies with the close of the long Acheh War in northern Sumatra. Secondly, the great technological advances in the West gave the new alien rulers of South-East Asia far greater ability to penetrate and alter traditional village society than any previous overlord had possessed. The introduction of modern communications, health services, commerce and transport meant that the changes experienced in the next decades were greater than had taken place in earlier centuries. Let us consider some of the most salient features of this transition.

In the first place, the impact of a money economy and the increasing endeavours of colonial commercial interests to control and develop the production and export of primary agricultural products had profound effects on the rural populations of the region. The development of cash

6 An Indonesian coffee plantation in the late nineteenth century. European enterprises like this gradually transformed traditional social and economic patterns.

crops combined with increased pressure on the land from the introduction of new standards of health and sanitation caused substantial changes in traditional village subsistence and communal land patterns. The earlier system of communal ownership broke down with the development of export crops and by the 1930s it had all but disappeared in most of the colonies. The relationship of the villager to his land was further modified by two other developments. Increased demands for agricultural exports and population pressure resulted in the opening of new lands in the deltas of Burma, Thailand and Indo-China, as well as on the outer islands of the Indies. The movement of people to new and unfamiliar areas intensified the disintegration of village norms already begun by the decline of communal ownership. Added to this was the growth of plantation agriculture which transformed villagers into members of an agricultural proletariat completely dependent on the money economy. The most vicious phase of these developments occurred in the inter-war years as the villager became increasingly dependent upon the world export economy and the fluctuations in the prices of unstable primary products. Thus more and more villagers fell into debt, with the increasing danger of the loss of their land. While this deterioration of the peasant economy was inhibited in some colonies, such as the Indies (where new land could not be owned by foreigners), it reached its worst in Burma, where by the end of the depression of the 1930s over half the cultivated land of Lower Burma was owned by Indian money-lenders. Thus land, which had been one of the strong threads in the fabric of village unity, lost much of its old relationship to traditional life in large areas of South-East Asia.

A second major factor in the changed conditions of the villager brought about by the penetration of Western technology was the introduction of new health standards. Since this was accompanied by the establishment of internal peace within the colonies and by developments in agriculture and transport which alleviated the danger of famine, the result was a major population explosion. The population of the island of Java jumped from 28 million in 1900 to 40 million in 1930, going on to reach over 65 million in 1970. In Burma it rose from approximately 10,400,000 in 1901 to 14,600,000 in 1931 and over 30 million today. The population of the Philippines increased by over 250 per cent in half a century and in Malaysia the advance was greater. The results were increased demands on land, the movement of people to cities and new lands, and new strains on a traditional social structure struggling to keep pace.

The deliberate or incidental results of the policies of the colonial powers with regard to village administration further weakened the social fabric of the villages, though in this respect there were considerable local variations. In Laos, some of the outer islands of Indonesia and Thailand the central government only slowly made incremental changes in local administration and did not move to destroy traditional relationships between the villager and administrator. Most important, in these areas recognized local leaders continued to maintain at least symbolic rule. In other areas, however, especially in Java, Burma proper and parts of Vietnam, the colonial administrators broke the thread of traditional government. Either through the direct rule of Europeans or through the interference of the colonial governments in the choice of local administrators, a new system was established based upon foreign laws and governors unfamiliar to the villager. In their desire to rule efficiently and remove what they considered to be undesirable customs and unsatisfactory native leaders, the colonial

7 Rangoon street scene. Increasing population brought with it an enlargement of the urban proletariat.

8 Opening of the King Edward VII College of Medicine, Singapore, 1926. New health standards led to a dramatic rise in population figures almost everywhere in South-East Asia.

rulers established an administrative apparatus towards which the villager felt little loyalty and within which the old and familiar ties of unity and legitimacy were broken.

Other areas in which the Western impact had a deleterious influence on the traditional social fabric were religion and education.[1] In the past the ruler and religion had been closely interrelated. In states such as Burma and Thailand the monarch had appointed the Buddhist patriarch and the court was clearly identified with the religious hierarchy. In Indonesia, Islam had penetrated to a large degree through the efforts of converted rulers, and Islam had always accepted a close relationship between religion and politics. Of considerable importance, furthermore, was the fact that the pre-colonial governments had regarded education as a prerogative of the religious. In the Theravada Buddhist countries of South-East Asia the monks were responsible for training the young men and most boys received a basic education under their tutelage. In the Islamic states a similar, if less extensive, role was played by Moslem teachers. After the colonial conquest both these threads were broken. The colonial governments either remained officially neutral regarding religion, as did the British and Americans, actively proselytized, as did the Spanish, or wavered, dependent upon pressures from the metropolitan countries, as did the French and Dutch. In any case the colonial ruler of the country was no longer a mentor of the same faith as his subjects, except in the Philippines (which had been converted to Christianity) and in independent Thailand. He was able to provide neither the spiritual foundation for government nor the necessary leadership to the religious structures of the polity.

In education the pattern was much the same. The colonial administrator and entrepreneur had little use for an education that emphasized the learning of religious scriptures by rote in Pali or Arabic. For them and for those seeking upwards mobility in a colonial society it was better to learn law or commerce in Dutch, English or French, all of which were taught best in Christian missionary schools and Western universities. Thus the religious hierarchy not only saw its traditional educational role decline, but lost its prerogatives to the purveyors of the conqueror's religion. In addition, therefore, the villager experienced a further deterioration of traditional ties to his village and social order.

The development of missionary education was only part of the expanding horizon opening out for those South-East Asians who were becoming more aware of the world around them. They were, of course, only a minority. The rural areas remained largely isolated from external

9 St Mary's Girls' School, Rangoon, established by the Society for the Propagation of the Gospel. An education at such a European school rapidly became almost a *sine qua non* for the Asian who aspired to a successful administrative career.

intellectual influences, and awareness of the outside world was primarily an urban phenomenon. The result, as we shall see later, was that those who learnt more of the outside world found themselves in an anomalous position, for the closer their contact with the West the more they became isolated from the views of their own people. Colonial régimes might allow the student to travel to Holland, England or France where he might chance upon other South-East Asians, but he could not travel to neighbouring countries in the area. Thus intellectuals in the region began to learn more of Molière, Shakespeare, Marx, Jefferson and Erasmus and less of the histories and traditional cultures of their own neighbours.

Yet, with minor exceptions in Indo-China, the colonial régimes did allow their subjects to study abroad, primarily in the metropolitan powers' own universities. Thus future politicians and nationalists of all the colonial countries journeyed abroad – to see political freedoms practised in the mother country which were prohibited in the colony and to learn of the ideas of liberal democrats, nationalists and revolutionaries such as Marx, Lenin, Hitler, Jefferson, Sun Yat Sen and Gandhi. These new ideas called into question not only the policies of the colonial régime but, of perhaps even greater long-term importance, they challenged many of the traditions of their respective societies. Thus the Communists used Lenin and other Socialist writers to decry both colonialism and religion, Sukarno claimed spiritual direction from Lenin, Hitler and Christ in support of Indonesian nationalism and Rizal pointed to liberal Spanish opinion in demanding both greater freedom from Spain and the victory of secularism over Church domination in the Philippines. Within the more religiously oriented leadership intellectual horizons were also broadened through modern communications and transport. Increasing numbers of pilgrims from South-East Asia to Mecca and Middle Eastern centres of learning brought both scholars and laymen in contact with modernist Islamic thought, which challenged traditional Malay and Indonesian customs and practices. Buddhist politicans such as U Nu and Moslem nationalists such as Harsono Tjokroaminoto and Agus Salim sought to synthesize Western Socialist theory with traditional religious values. The heterogeneous character of religion in Vietnam led to fascinating efforts to interweave local values with Western secular thought and tenets of Catholicism best epitomized by the highly syncretic Cao Dai faith. While many of the ideas of Western intellectuals failed to permeate rural areas, some of the new religious thought did do so; and the first four decades of this century saw new ferment in both rural and urban South-East Asia.

20

While economic, social, political and intellectual changes were taking place in the towns and villages of the region, the West was generating major changes in the very nature of national government. Of central importance was the formation of the very states which were to inhabit South-East Asia in the post-war era. While the pre-colonial kingdoms in Burma, Cambodia and Vietnam had controlled much of the territory which was later organized as a colony, the final borders of these states were largely drawn by the Europeans. The impact of the West on nation-building was most obvious, however, in peninsular Malaya and the island archipelagos. The former had been composed of warring principalities until British colonial rule conquered and cajoled the peninsula into a single state. The Philippines had been even less united, lacking religious, historical or linguistic unity until Spanish colonial rule welded the islands into a state and then a nation. In spite of efforts many centuries earlier to expand the empires of Sjrivijaya and Mahjapahit, no Indonesian had ever ruled what was to be the Dutch East Indies. It is interesting to note that after independence the major argument presented by the Indonesian government for the incorporation of West Irian into the new state was that it had been part of the old Dutch colonial empire (although differing in culture, race and history from the rest of the archipelago).

Within these European-formed boundaries a new political, social and economic order was being established. While it did not reach all the people within the colony (most of the European powers exercised control over the hinterlands of their domains for less than fifty years) the colonial system did markedly change old forms and institutions. We have noted the most salient ways in which penetration by the West changed the traditional society of the region. We may now consider what kind of society had resulted from that transformation by the time of the last full decade of colonial rule in the 1930s.

COLONIAL POLITICAL PATTERNS

The political-administrative systems established by the various colonial governments varied across the region in three basic ways: the type of administrative apparatus, the amount of autonomy accorded to the colony, and the degree of political freedom allowed to their subjects. Administratively, the two most important differences were related to the employment of direct and indirect rule. Direct rule, that is the administration of an area directly through European- or government-selected Asian civil servants, was practised by the Dutch throughout almost all of Java and

Madura, by the British in lowland Burma, by the French in what is now Vietnam, and by the Spanish and Americans in most of the Philippine Islands. This system brought the populace into direct contact with the colonial administration with no buffer of traditional authority and legitimacy. It also tended to necessitate a larger government apparatus, but it was argued that it was nevertheless a more effective means of developing the region. In contrast, indirect rule followed the principle of retaining the local ruler in at least a symbolic role, under the guidance and tutelage of a representative of the central government. This pattern was followed in the outer islands of the Dutch East Indies, and in the hill areas of Burma, Cambodia, Laos and the sultanates of British Malaya. The amount of European control varied from region to region and tended to increase in time – particularly in the East Indies, where efforts to combat depression brought the Dutch administration more directly to bear. Supporters of indirect rule argued that it necessitated the employment of fewer Europeans, gave greater legitimacy to government decisions and defused anti-colonial attacks by putting the local ruler between the people and European administration. In addition, under indirect rule the native rulers were

10–11 Below, indirect rule: the sultan of Kedah; such local rulers were permitted to retain a symbolic role under the central government. Opposite left, direct rule: a Dutch governor of Samarang in central Java, 1904; the Dutch denied all political responsibility to the local people of their colonies in the region.

dependent upon the colonial government for continued support and thus felt more loyalty to the mother country.

As noted, this type of rule affected the size of the civil service, but the racial character of those who staffed the administration was important as well. In the British colonies the tendency was to keep down the number of Europeans, particularly after the First World War. Burmese found themselves employed at all levels of government including the higher reaches of the civil service, the executive council and, by the mid-1930s, the premiership. Of course, the British continued to hold key positions in defence, the police and finance and, as in other colonies, those Burmese who had enjoyed a missionary education found it easier to advance than those who had not. The Americans were even more anxious to divest themselves of the administration of their South-East Asian colony than the British and within a generation of its conquest over 90 per cent of the administrative posts were held by Filipinos. On the other hand, both France and the Netherlands employed large numbers of Europeans in civil administration, and the French were particularly known for having brought about the presence of a French administrative proletariat in Vietnam. Even after the

12 Soon after acquiring Cuba and the Philippines, the United States – here trying to teach self-government – had grown anxious to divest itself of the administration of its South-East Asia colony. The cartoon depicts Emilio Aguinaldo, the Filipino who led a revolt against the US, in a dunce's cap, while Cuba fights it out in front.

Second World War Frenchmen were performing police and clerical functions that had long been left to locals in other colonies. While Indonesians and Vietnamese were employed at most levels of administration they tended to find it considerably more difficult to rise to positions of responsibility. In part this was due to nationalist boycotts against co-operating with the colonial government, but it also reflected a lack of French confidence in the ability and loyalty of the educated locals.

The second major area of difference lay in the amount of real autonomy from the metropolitan power secured by the colony. One index of this was the degree to which South-East Asians were able to participate in colonial politics. But autonomy could also mean simply that the colonial administration had far greater freedom of action. In fact, by the 1930s almost all the colonies had their own legislative councils with varying percentages of Asian members, local tax powers and, within limits, some flexibility in administering the day-to-day operations of the colony. In each case, however, the chief administrator and representative of the colonial government had a power of veto over the local legislature, and the governments of London, Paris, The Hague and Washington maintained ultimate decision-making authority over their colonies. There were, of course, distinct differences in the degree of autonomy allowed between the colonial régimes, a progression from freedom to restriction starting with the United States and continuing through the United Kingdom and the Netherlands to France. These variations were to be seen in the taxing powers of the colony, the extent to which the governor exercised his veto, the powers granted to the legislative body and the degree of interference in colonial policies practised by legislatures of the home country. The existence of one area of autonomy did not guarantee the existence of another and there were notable changes in the last years of colonial rule under the pressure of the depression, nationalism and the exigencies of the Second World War.

The issue which has received the greatest post-war consideration has been the amount of political freedom allowed to the colonial peoples. Although there has been much controversy over both fact and interpretation, there is now a broad area of agreement. On the whole, there is little doubt that the United States was most liberal, followed by the United Kingdom, the Netherlands and France in that order. By the mid-1930s the United States had agreed to the independence of the Philippines within a decade and had meanwhile accepted a Filipino legislature and executive, with the chief representative of the United States displaying considerable restraint in the use of his reserve powers. Political parties were allowed to compete, basic civil rights were granted and political expression was freer than anywhere else in East Asia at that time.

During this same period Burma was moving swiftly towards self-government, using the concessions granted to India as a basis for progress. The majority of the legislature and executive council were Burmese, and so after 1936 was the premier. Political parties competed and their news-papers strongly criticized the colonial régime. The basic differences. between the British and the American positions were that in British colonies independence or full Commonwealth status was in the indefinite future and that the governor's reserve powers and colonial administrative role were more apparent. Without a clear promise of complete freedom, radical nationalists were more prepared to take strong measures, which resulted in counter-measures by the government restricting some forms of political expression. However, until the onset of the Second World War in Europe and the adoption of stringent defence policies by the British, Burma was one of the least restricted colonies in Afro-Asia.

For a decade after the beginning of the First World War the Dutch East Indies were in the forefront of political reform in South-East Asia. National-ist organizations, including after 1920 the Indonesian Communist Party, vigorously engaged in party and labour activity. Newspapers and pamphlets openly and strongly debated public issues, and the beginnings of local participation in the colony's decision-making process were made with the establishment of the Volksraad, a national legislative assembly with restricted powers. While the government was not prepared to allow full political freedom (and European radicals in particular were quickly exiled from the colony), the Indies appeared to be developing in the direc-tion followed by the Philippines and Burma. The growth of nationalist violence culminating in a short-lived Communist-led revolt in 1926–27, however, combined with the economic devastation of the depression, im-pelled the Dutch towards a policy of repression. By the 1930s the Indies were far behind the American and British colonies in the area of political freedom. Representative Indonesians were a minority in the Volksraad, which in any case had not fulfilled its early promise. Political parties were restricted and later leaders of independent Indonesia such as Sukarno and Sjharir were arrested and exiled for nationalist activities. Few Indonesians found themselves in positions of real authority and the Dutch maintained heavily paternalistic policies in what one British scholar-civil servant termed a 'hot-house' atmosphere.[2]

13 French lady in a rickshaw in late nineteenth-century Indo-China. The arrival of European women and children in South-East Asia produced greater aloofness on the part of the colonists and inflamed racial tensions.

Without question, however, it was in the French colonies that political freedom was at its lowest ebb in inter-war South-East Asia. Even moderate evolutionary nationalists found themselves in danger of imprisonment and the 'Red Terror' of radical nationalists was met by the 'White Terror' of French repression. While the death penalty was rarely imposed against nationalists in the other colonial territories it was common in Vietnam. Nowhere in Indo-China was there an effective elected national legislature with a majority of local representatives. Political parties found it difficult to operate and political expression was sharply curtailed. At the same time there were considerable variations within the French dominions. In Laos and Cambodia organized nationalist activity had never succeeded in mobilizing mass support and the French had few problems with minor court intrigues. In what is now Vietnam organized political activity existed only in urban areas and in Cochin-China, and even that was severely restricted. Political activity in Indo-China thus tended to be engaged in through underground, conspiratorial and revolutionary channels. As Ellen Hammer has noted, 'by declaring political opposition illegal and subject to police reprisals, the administration left nationalists who desired action no alternative but to operate clandestinely, as revolutionaries.'[3]

The social order of pre-war South-East Asia has been described as a dual society in which the modernized European was ranged against the more traditional indigenous population. In actuality society in the region was usually composed of several tiers. The majority of villagers were outside the reach of regular European influence and tended to remain static; major changes only came about in the post-war years. Elsewhere, there were basically three social tiers, the indigenous masses participating in the colonial system, the Asian élite, and the Europeans.

In most colonies an increasingly wide chasm had opened between the Europeans and Asians during the nineteenth and early twentieth centuries. When the foreigners had first arrived, there had been few apparent differences between them and their new subjects in terms of education and the tools they employed. In some areas, indeed, such as agriculture and education, there was much to learn from the Asian (it is reported that when the British first occupied Burma there was a higher rate of literacy among the Burmese than existed in the United Kingdom). But, as the Industrial Revolution made its impact on the West, important differences began to appear between the élites of the two regions. The Europeans became proficient in engineering, modern agriculture, hygiene, transportation and other specialties, which were not to be introduced into Asian education until late in the colonial era. This gave the colonial rulers a clear superiority in technique over their subjects and increased the disparity between the two. As the Europeans expanded their roles from merchant rulers into developers and administrators colonial society was further changed by the increasing number of European families settling in the colonies. Previously, single males arrived in South-East Asia, took part in native society and often lived with Asian women (as evidenced by the sizable Indo-, Anglo- and other mixed-blood population of several countries in the region). The development of a European society including larger numbers of women and children, however, led to an increasing isolation from the local population and greater racial tension. This pattern was epitomized in the region by the European clubs where the whites felt safe and aloof from the 'natives'. Described beautifully in George Orwell's *Burmese Days*, the club was the 'spiritual citadel', the 'Nirvana for which native officials and millionaires pine in vain'.[4] Some clubs had signs prohibiting dogs and

Asians, others began to admit a few 'safe' indigenous aristocrats or civil servants, but over-all they represented the racial character of the last decades of colonial rule. The membership rolls of clubs cast light on the process of social change. One golf club in Burma, for example, lists none but European officers and trophy-winners up to the Japanese occupation. After the war, however, Burmese names appear and the club was ultimately entirely run by them. In other countries clubs remained dominated by expatriates long after independence.

In some colonies there was a local élite which was Western-trained and socially acceptable, within limits. When indigenous sultans, sawbwas and other aristocrats maintained at least symbolic power, they not only retained traditional social status but were among the first to gain the educational advantages offered by the West. Thus the anomalous situation often arose in which a Western-educated ruler was addressed by social inferiors in the special high court language of the particular region; and on another level we have the official portrait of a group of Indonesian nationalists studying in Holland in which everyone is dressed in morning coats! For those without traditional family status or wealth, education and Christianity offered the means of upwards mobility within the colonial system. Although few Buddhists or Moslems were prepared to convert to the ruler's faith, many did take advantage of his missionary schools. For those that did convert there was greater ease in gaining government posts, although this may have been tied to the training they had received. In the French colonies in particular, an individual educated in the French tradition and professing Catholicism enjoyed major advantages in the colonial society.

There is no doubt that greater attention was given in the inter-war years to the question of closing the educational and social gaps between Europeans and Asians. Clubs began to open their doors to non-Europeans, local institutions of higher learning were opened in most colonies, more Asians were allowed to go overseas for education, and some efforts were made to diminish racial conflict. The process was slow and halting, however, and by no means universal. In most of South-East Asia literacy in the colonial language was less than 20 per cent, the lowest rates being in Indo-China and the East Indies. But the teaching of the colonial language was repudiated by many nationalists who sought to establish national schools in the local language. Higher education was for a very small élite, many of whom came from the aristocratic families. Furthermore, justice was not equal, since equal punishment for crimes was not normal between Asian and European.

14 Hanoi cathedral, 1926. The benefits to be gained through professing the colonial ruler's faith inevitably undermined the authority of traditional religious leaders.

From the economic point of view the two salient forces aiding the growth of nationalism were probably the entrance of commercial agriculture and the increasing pressure of Chinese and Indian entrepreneurs. As has been noted, commercial agriculture made the peasant more dependent upon the fluctuations of the world market. It also made him more aware of being under the control of forces outside his own village. It was not Lenin's explanation of imperialism as the last stage of capitalism that galvanized him into anti-colonial activity, but his inability to cope with the vagaries of the colonial economy and the demands of the Asian money-lenders. The plantation worker in particular was made more aware of his dependence on the European and of the disparity between his own condition and that of the management. As the South-East Asian found himself losing his land or business to the foreigner or was driven into membership of an agricultural or industrial proletariat, the words of the young nationalists became more persuasive.

This is clearly borne out by the location of the main centres of pre-war nationalist activity. In Burma it was in Rangoon, in the new lands of the delta where the Chettyar money-lenders had taken the peasants' land and among the small industrialized working class of the oil-fields that nationalism was rife. In the Indies nationalism grew in the urban centres where unions such as that of the transport workers were active, in Central Java, where the penetration of the Chinese endangered traditional Indonesian control of the batik industry, and in plantation areas such as the country around Medan in northern Sumatra. In the Philippines, apart from Manila, early anti-Spanish activities centred in areas where land was owned by the Spanish religious Orders, and when violence later broke out in Luzon inequities in land-holding were the target. Nor is it surprising that nationalism was often connected with anti-Indian or anti-Chinese disturbances, for while the Europeans might control the national economy, the non-indigenous Asian was the day-to-day symbol of economic exploitation. Thus there were anti-Chinese riots in Thailand and violence against Indians in Burma in the 1930s which drew the support of nationalist leaders, and in the Indies various programmes initiated by the government against the Chinese received nationalist approval.

Social ingredients in the rise of nationalism varied from personal affronts by European wives to deep-seated religious antagonisms, but at the forefront were the disparities inherent in the dualism of colonial society and assertions of religious identity. The dual standards of colonial society provided a multitude of occasions to prick the sensitivities of the non-Europeans.

Racial discrimination was epitomized by the all-white clubs, but inequality in the administration of justice, the preference for Europeans in promotion to the better jobs and prejudice evinced in personal relations were all part of the racial character of the environment. These were apparent in every colony in spite of palliatives such as French assimilation, the knighthoods and honours conferred by the British on Burmese leaders, and the ritual obeisance given to Malay and Indonesian sultans. It should be noted, however, that the political impact of the dual society was generally centred in cities and towns and did not spread into most rural areas, where the European was seldom seen.

Of far greater universal significance was the factor of religious nationalism. Religion was an extremely complex element in the politics of twentieth-century colonial South-East Asia, but the most pervasive political forces within it were felt dangers to the faith, the role of religious leaders, the employment of traditional symbols, and religion as a unifying force against the colonial government.

The fact that in all but one of the colonies of the region the European ruler was of a different faith from his subjects became a rallying-cry for the religious nationalists. In Burma Buddhist monks decried the decline of morality under the British, and monk-politicans like U Ottuma argued that it was not possible to achieve Nirvana under Christian domination. In the Indies Moslems railed against the 'Kaffir' Dutch and policies which they believed reflected the Church politics of Holland. In Moslem and Buddhist colony alike there was criticism of the expanding role of Christian missionary education at the expense of traditional schooling.

The rule of the non-believer and the loss of old roles had a considerable impact on local religious leaders, many of whom sought to challenge colonial rule. Where previously Buddhist monks and Moslem ulamas and hadjis had counselled kings and princes, taught the young and been the standard-bearers of national values, they now found their places taken by Christian administrators and missionaries. Furthermore, the penetration of the region by Western values and technology resulted in the gradual secularization of colonial society, endangering the very core of religious doctrine. It was thus not surprising that mass nationalist organizations such as the Burmese General Council of Buddhist Associations and the Indonesian Sarekat Islam, as well as smaller political groups in Indo-China, found religious personnel taking central roles, nor that many of the violent protests against the colonial government and non-indigenous Asians were not without religious support and leadership.

15–18 The European impact. Above, a French official in Indo-China cheerfully symbolizes the racialism of the colonial Powers. Right, houses in Old Batavia, Java, showing unmistakable signs of Dutch influence. Inland rural areas, however, were penetrated by Westerners only sporadically or not at all: below, village scene in Java and (right) peasant women washing clothes in a river.

19 The ruins of Angkor Wat. Discovered by Europeans, such testimonies to a glorious past ironically helped to stimulate anti-colonial nationalist sentiment.

Religion could also supply more specific symbols against the foreigner. Throughout South-East Asia the tradition of a Messiah was continually brought forward to raise hopes of redemption or to clothe a rising politician. This expectation was employed widely by people as diverse as the leader of a mass party in the Indies and a Japanese officer invading British Burma. Of less consequence was the employment of animistic symbols for protection and success. At times these were tragically comical, as when anti-British rebels in Burma sought to prove their immunity from harm by painting targets on their rears and waving them at the colonial troops! (They did not prove successful.) All of these factors, however, had particular significance in South-East Asia because of the very heterogeneity of the countries involved. Religion could provide the one common bond in societies divided on most other bases. Thus, while Indonesia and the Philippines may have been formed as states by colonial administrations and lacked a single language, history or set of social customs, 90 per cent of their populations could claim one religious faith. This common belief linking a welter of communal groups was of even greater importance when the colonial régime professed a different faith.

34

All these forces helped to make the South-East Asian more aware of himself and of his heritage. New communications and technology brought him into contact with his fellow countrymen, and he began to think of himself as Indonesian rather than as Javanese or Padanger, as Vietnamese instead of Annamese or Tonkinese, or as Filipino rather than as a member of a small political entity. Efforts were made to develop and modernize the national language, and in Indonesia a new one was even formulated. The growth of religious nationalism strengthened the South-East Asian's sense of a common cause against the outside world, as the demands of European, Chinese and Indian entrepreneurs made him conscious of the pressures of the colonial economy and desirous of cutting himself free from its fetters. The racial and class environment of colonial life inflamed his sensitivity to injustice, while simultaneously European writers showed him what freedom and independence should and could be. Ironically the European rediscoveries of monuments such as the Borobadur on Java and Angkor Wat in Cambodia also helped to make the South-East Asian more aware of his own historic heritage. All these elements interacted to reinforce the feeling of identity. As one Indonesian nationalist commented, there were two classes in the Indies, the downtrodden Indonesian Moslems and the rich Dutch Christians.

To understand the impact of the interaction of colonialism and nationalism on later events it is useful to study one colony in greater depth. The Dutch East Indies, the largest and one of the oldest colonies in the region, experienced considerable change in the twentieth century. We have noted the rise of nationalism, early Dutch reform followed by political repression, the impact of the depression and the effects of direct and indirect rule in this most paternalistic of European domains. However, these generalizations hide the traumatic impact of the nature of colonial rule and the nationalist reaction.

The heterogeneous character of Indonesian society brought forward variegated nationalist responses to colonialism. Basically three streams arose, each with a multitude of tributaries. The broadest was the religious nationalist movement that claimed the first mass nationalist organization, Sarekat Islam. Religion could attract those unhappy with Christian rule and seeking their own identity, but it proved a weak bond in the long run. Islam in the Indies might include 90 per cent of the population, but it varied markedly across the archipelago in theory and practice. Within a decade of its height the movement fractured along traditional-modernist lines. Furthermore, the necessity for a national party to debate secular issues such as taxes, plantation labour and health led the faithful into internal dissension.

The second stream was secular nationalist, composed of those who believed that religion was part of the private lives of individuals and was too parochial and traditional to provide the foundation to a modern nation. Instead these young men espoused an ideology of democracy, independence, social justice and economic reform. While they never developed a mass base in the inter-war years, the secular nationalist parties spawned many leaders of independent Indonesia. At the same time they earned the animosity of both the religious parties and the Dutch administration.

The third stream was Socialist-Marxist in content and intermingled with the other two. Marxist thought had reached the Indies through Dutch Socialists in the years just prior to the First World War. There it found a fertile field when a local Communist party (the PKI) was formed in the early 1920s, and both the religious and secular nationalists included individuals deeply influenced by Socialist thinking. However, some of the more radical exponents of Marxism soon alienated traditional elements of Indonesian society, and when the PKI and its supporters seemed to attack the religious base of Sarekat Islam the lines were drawn. Thus, while the abortive PKI-led uprisings of 1926–27 destroyed the Communists as an effective organization for almost twenty years, the bitterness remained in the Moslem camp.

The result of this series of conflicts was a fragmented nationalist movement that from time to time made efforts to merge differences but was ultimately unable to agree on basic policy and ideological issues. Thus when the Japanese arrived there was no united party that could meet the challenges of the new situation.

This disunity was furthered by a conscious Dutch policy which after the mid-1920s aimed at the arrest and exile of those nationalists accused of speaking or acting against the peace and order of the colony. Those considered most dangerous were likely to find themselves exiled to the infamous Digoel prison camp in West Irian. Later they, like lesser political prisoners, might be sent to reside on a remote island. This meant that exiles such as Sukarno and Sjharir were given little opportunity to develop the skills necessary to administer a large territory like Indonesia or to compete in a democratic environment. Sukarno spent almost the entire decade before the Japanese invasions in exile from the political life of the colony.

This political repression at the hands of the Dutch also led many trained Indonesians to refuse to co-operate with the colonial administration by accepting positions in it – Sukarno himself took a degree in engineering that he never used. This not only cut the Dutch off from trained people who might have provided a bridgehead to the general population, but it further reduced the number of Indonesians with administrative experience which they could have employed when independence finally arrived.

It would leave the reader with an inaccurate picture of the impact of nationalism in the region if it were not emphasized that as of the late 1930s nationalist ferment was by no means universal. Much of rural South-East Asia still remained isolated from the political currents of the day and uninterested in what was happening outside their villages. In the areas under indirect rule, antagonisms and loyalties tended to be directed towards the local traditional ruler, who generally supported the colonial government. Christian groups indeed, such as the Karens of Burma and the Amboinese in the Indies, outspokenly declared their loyalty to the British and Dutch respectively. In Laos, Cambodia and Malaya expressions of nationalism were rare during the inter-war years and the masses were apolitical.

Modern nationalism in South-East Asia primarily grew out of a reaction to the colonial system and its impact on the social and economic fabric of a people in transition. Its growth cannot simply be ascribed to a reaction to foreign rule, and to attribute its rise to a single cause such as capitalism or tyrannical colonial administration would be to misrepresent the complicated interaction of a multitude of forces alluded to in our previous analysis. No doubt a central element was anger and alienation resulting from rule by a foreign power that viewed its role as a combination of saviour and exploiter of colonies desirable for prestige, military strength and commercial value. But it must also be remembered that the confrontation between the European and his subjects took place during a period of changing horizons in South-East Asia, when new intellectual, economic and social challenges were making the Asian more aware of himself and his actions.

We have noted in passing the widening horizons of many Asians, particularly in the urban centres. It is important also to consider how the penetration of new ideas influenced nationalist thinking. The impact on Asian intellectuals of Western political writers and events elsewhere in Asia has often been noted. There is little doubt that leaders such as U Nu, Sukarno and Ho Chi Minh were fascinated by both liberal democratic and Marxist thought. Their early speeches are peppered with references to evolutionary Socialists such as the Fabians, revolutionaries such as Lenin, nationalists of varying shades such as Mazzini, the Sinn Fein, or Hitler, and liberal democrats such as Jefferson. Occasionally a nationalist of the temper of Sjharir would be so overwhelmed by Western thought that he would fill his writings with Huizinga, Ortega y Gasset and Croce, while showing an almost total absence of any Asian influence.[5] Furthermore, the victory of Japan in the Russo-Japanese War and the later activities of Sun Yat Sen in China made some young nationalists more aware of the possibilities open to Asians in their challenge to seemingly entrenched power.

Without the coincidental widening of the horizons of other elements of the population, however, there is considerable doubt whether the words of the Western-oriented nationalists would have found a receptive audience. What they did encounter was a people in flux. Modern technology, colonial administration and commercial agriculture were beginning to break down traditional village loyalties and to increase contact among previously isolated groups of people. Where the peasant had once been cognizant only of the area around his village, owing allegiance primarily to his family and only dimly aware of a larger polity, he was now slowly being brought into a wider commercial and administrative system in which his traditional social and political ties were being seriously eroded.

20 Ho Chi Minh at the French Socialist Congress at Tours, 1920. By allowing their subjects to study abroad, the colonial Powers brought Asian intellectuals into contact with progressive Western thought, thus sowing the seeds of their own downfall.

2 The Legacy of the Second World War

The Second World War affected South-East Asia in two stages, the war in Europe and the Japanese invasion. The German occupation of Holland and France and the threatened invasion of the United Kingdom had an important, but not decisive, influence on events and institutions in the region. For the British colonies, and particularly Burma, it meant greater surveillance of the nationalists and the paying of more attention to local defence needs. The former resulted in the arrest of a number of Burmese nationalist leaders who were considered dangerous to the colonial government. These comprised both older politicians, including two premiers, and young firebrands such as the later Prime Minister, U Nu. At the same time there were efforts to placate the politically aware Burmese in the light of the danger of a widening war. The economies of Burma and Malaya were not badly disrupted, since the former's rice exports were directed elsewhere and the latter substituted other markets for her products. But the importation of necessary European goods was, of course, severely curtailed.

A somewhat similar situation existed in the Dutch East Indies, although there 'radical' nationalists had already been detained or exiled. During the war, however, renewed efforts were made to arrive at an agreement as to the political future of the colony and proposals for a type of commonwealth status were discussed. These attempts remained abortive at the time of the Japanese occupation in December 1941. Although ties with Holland were broken by the German occupation of that country, formal links remained with the government in exile in London, to which the colonial administration remained loyal. As a substitute for the traditional trade with Europe increased exports were sent to the United States, which was developing its own war potential and needed the islands' tin and rubber. Otherwise, things were largely as before.

It was in the French colonies that European events had their greatest impact. With the fall of France and establishment of the Vichy régime the colonial administration in Indo-China had to decide where its loyalty lay.

It chose Vichy. Allied control of the seas therefore all but cut the colony off from effective ties with the mother country, and the French in South-East Asia felt more isolated than did the Dutch or British. Without financial or military support the colony became highly vulnerable to increasing Japanese demands. Little political freedom had been granted to the indigenous inhabitants prior to the war, but as a result of events in Europe a number of nationalists who had decided to remain above ground were arrested and some were executed. In the short period between the German occupation of France and the Japanese occupation of Indo-China little was done to change the political role of the local population.

The Japanese movement into South-East Asia had considerably more far-reaching consequences.[1] Even before the final invasion of the region began on 8 December 1941, the Japanese had attempted to project their power. There had, of course, been imperial agents in Thailand and the colonies in the 1930s; but there were more critical pressures prior to the war. One was through contacts with dissident young nationalists, especially in Burma, where the Japanese recruited men who were to play a major role in the nation's future. In 1941 a Japanese agent in Rangoon gathered thirty men for military training abroad. Some joined in the hope of fulfilling personal ambitions, while others were active nationalists. In time they be-

21 The surrender of Singapore, 1942. The colonial Powers never recovered from the 'loss of face' that followed the success of the Japanese invasion.

came the legendary 'Thirty Comrades', who swore a blood oath in Thailand and later went to Taiwan for training. These men were to return to Burma to fight the British in the cause of independence. Their actions as a group had little impact on the outcome of the war, but past membership in the 'Thirty Comrades' became political treasure for men such as Aung San, Father of Burmese independence, and Ne Win, later commander of free Burma's armed forces and now its ruler.

Economic pressures were also instituted by Japan, in an effort to gain favourable terms of trade and access to the raw materials necessary for the nation's military and industrial development. Bargaining in this area was long and hard as Japan sought to take advantage of the greater vulnerability of the Dutch and French. In the case of the Indies the Dutch negotiators were able to frustrate Japan's hopes.

It was in Indo-China that Japan opened the first deep crack in the foundations of colonialism in South-East Asia. In this case the French were forced to make concessions never previously granted to an Asian power. Incapable of defending itself against Japanese demands, the Vichy government had but 50,000 French troops and 120 planes in Indo-China. An abortive effort to gain American support was met with the advice to acquiesce and only the Pétain régime in France counselled taking up arms. After a short engagement on land against small elements of nationalists and a sea war with the Thais, the French were forced to capitulate on Japanese terms. Ultimately territory was surrendered to the Thais, but the Japanese were allowed to maintain troops in Indo-China and products were exported to Japan in exchange for blocked yen. In return the French were able to maintain their colonial administration, police force and military largely intact. This was the first major loss of face for the Europeans, but ironically the French maintained symbolic and considerable real power over their subjects longer than any other colonial government in South-East Asia, since the Japanese allowed them to keep control until March 1945.

Once the war began the Japanese occupation of South-East Asia was relatively swift. Thailand agreed to become an ally and Thai soil became a launching zone for attacks on Malaya and Burma. Although an anti-Japanese 'Free Thai' movement was formed in Washington and London the country remained fundamentally untouched by the war except for shortages of goods. Imperial forces moved swiftly down the Malay Peninsula, capturing Kuala Lumpur on 11 January 1942 and accepting the surrender of supposedly impregnable Singapore on 15 February 1942. In Burma the apparently inevitable took somewhat longer, for Commonwealth troops fought a rearguard action. Nevertheless Rangoon had been taken by early March and by May Mandalay had fallen as the Allied troops escaped to India. Burma was to remain under Japanese control for the duration, and it was not until 5 May 1945 that British-led units reoccupied Rangoon.

The imperial forces waited until the fall of Singapore before launching their invasion of the Indies, but after a series of disastrous naval engagements the Dutch capitulated on 8 March 1942, having carried out a scorched-earth policy but having offered comparatively little resistance on land. Apart from small areas on New Guinea no island in the colony was retaken until after the Japanese surrender in August 1945. The Philippines held out the longest: the invasion there began soon after 8 December and Manila was declared an open city on 2 January 1942. American and Filipino units retreated to the Bataan Peninsula, where they held out until 9 April 1942, shortly after which the island stronghold of Corregidor capitulated. Although the Filipino command called for the surrender of all units on 8 May 1942, guerrilla bands were to harass the Japanese until MacArthur's return in 1944. However, within approximately six months of the Japanese attack on Pearl Harbor on 7 December 1941 no major armed resistance remained from northern Luzon to Indonesia and from the Indian border to western New Guinea.

In most cases the Japanese were inferior in number to the troops they were facing and the Asians witnessed mass surrenders of their former masters on Luzon, at Singapore and in the Indies. In places such as Penang and Rangoon they noted the flight of European families, leaving the native population to face the mercies of the Japanese. In Indo-China the French accepted imperial overlordship as a condition for remaining in nominal control. In short, the Japanese invasion was a military and political disaster for the colonial powers, who would never again feel complete masters of their territories in South-East Asia. The profound changes which ensued during the next three years can be examined under three rubrics, the 'loss of face' of the Europeans, Japanese political aid to independence movements, and the ending of the colonial powers' monopoly of modern weapons.

The impact of the so-called 'loss of face' was felt in many areas. The fact that the colonial governments were incapable of defending their subjects called into question their right to rule. The sight of white soldiers rather meekly surrendering, being sent on long marches to prison camps in which many collapsed along the road and later being herded into forced-labour

22 The myth of colonial omnipotence exposed: British prisoners prepare their main meal of rice in the cookhouse at Changi gaol, Singapore.

projects such as the infamous Burma–Thai 'railroad of death' may have elicited sympathy for the individuals from those watching but it did not reflect omnipotent colonial power. In addition the rounding-up of colonial administrators, merchants, planters and professional men and their families established an entirely new environment which was free from the old masters and lacked the racialist tone which had characterized colonial society. Europeans behind camp walls were dependent upon friendly Asians for extra food and other necessities. Perhaps most important of all, the new power in the region was a fellow Asian who in the initial euphoria of victory appeared to many as a liberator from colonial oppression.

Of central additional importance were the Japanese programmes designed to move the occupied territories closer to independence and to increase nationalist awareness. These were not fully initiated by Japan immediately, however, and it is open to question whether the government in Tokyo really intended to offer independence as soon as it did. It is more likely that increasing internal pressure from local nationalists and the need to gain public support in the light of Allied victories accelerated the process. Certainly the Greater East Asian Co-Prosperity Sphere did not initially envisage totally free and independent nations within it and probably Japan hoped to establish submissive states on the model of Manchukuo.

After the first enthusiasm over the defeat of the colonial powers had worn off, the Japanese new order encountered increasing dissatisfaction in its South-East Asian domains. There were those who were never prepared to accept the Japanese. Many people in the Chinese communities were well aware of the atrocity stories that had accompanied the invasion of China and were understandably worried about their future. Christians in Burma and Indonesia had formed close ties with the British and Dutch and saw in their defeat an impairment of their own status. Both the Japanese and the nationalists were suspicious of their loyalty – and correctly so in Burma where many Christians aided Allied military activities. For the remainder of South-East Asia the Co-Prosperity Sphere developed into something less than had been expected. The disruption of old trade patterns and the increasingly successful Allied blockade produced severe economic dislocations and the disappearance of Western goods to which the urban populations had become accustomed. Maintaining an automobile in working order became a test of mechanical ingenuity if petrol was available, and even cloth and food became scarce.

These shortages would have been accepted by many as necessary sacrifices for independence had it not been for Japanese tardiness in offering freedom. They did release political prisoners from exile and jail, it is true, and Europeans were eliminated from positions of responsibility except in rare instances where their skills were temporarily necessary. Yet the new rulers displayed some of the same superiority seen in the former colonial systems, as epitomized by Tojo's instructions to the Japanese forces to 'respect the opinions of the natives and to take a true, fatherly attitude towards them'. It was not until the last two years of the war that even symbolic independence was granted to Indonesia, Burma and the Philippines, while the Indo-Chinese states had to wait until after March 1945. Nevertheless real changes did take place in South-East Asia during the war years.

The tendency among outside observers of the time was to regard the Japanese-supported régimes as mere puppets and their leaders as quislings or men of weak character. There is little doubt that these governments were denied full responsibility for their affairs and that Japanese civil and military authorities maintained the ultimate power of veto to the end. In military matters the representatives of Tokyo were supreme and efforts were made to control the wartime economy. Yet South-East Asians were

23 Like others of the post-war nationalist leaders in South-East Asia, President Sukarno (seen here on one of his last appearances as Indonesian Head of State) obtained his first taste of power under the Japanese occupation.

to be found at all levels of the civil administration, where they acquired the experience often denied them by colonial governments. Whereas there was little change in the racial composition of the administrative élite in the Philippines, indigenous personnel took over in Burma, Indonesia and Indo-China. Dr Ba Maw, first premier under the British, became the war-time ruler of Burma. Found politically and personally unacceptable by the younger nationalists, he did not outlast the war, but some of his colleagues, such as General Aung San and Information and Foreign Minister U Nu, were to lead post-war governments.[2] In Indonesia the Japanese-supported régime was headed by President Sukarno, who was to rule after independence for more than two decades, and many of the military men who succeeded him in power served under the occupation. In the few months of full Japanese control of Vietnam neither Ho Chi Minh of the North nor Ngo Dinh Diem of the South participated in the government, but Emperor Bao Dai was made its titular head. In Cambodia the young Norodom Sihanouk had been ruling monarch since 1941 and was to continue to lead his country until 1970. Even in the Philippines some of those supposedly tainted with the brush of collaboration were later reinstated into political

45

life, though the wartime president, José Laurel, was arrested and imprisoned for a period. Only in the two countries retaken by the Allies before the war's end, Burma and the Philippines, were the leaders deposed permanently. Thus a new post-war élite arose from the occupation, an élite generally considered as honourable nationalists by their people, an élite now somewhat better qualified to rule than had been true previously.

Not only did the wartime period spawn new leaders; in some cases it saw the formation of political and social organizations which were to outlast the conflict. In Burma was born the Anti-Fascist People's Freedom League (AFPFL) which was to rule Burma for some fifteen years. During this period there were also efforts to unite the fragmented Buddhist hierarchy and diminish the secularism which characterized the colonial system. In Indonesia new political and religious organizations burgeoned, although the traditional splits in the nationalist movement were not permanently mended by wartime co-operation. In Malaya the Chinese guerrilla movement developed strong Communist leanings which provided the foundation for post-war anti-colonial activities, while in Vietnam the Viet Minh was developing along similar lines. In sum then, this was not a period of stagnation, since the forced withdrawal of the colonial administrations opened new opportunities for the people of South-East Asia.

The Japanese played an active part in promoting anti-colonialist sentiment from the beginning, casting themselves in the role of liberators, fellow Asians and, to the Buddhists in the region, co-religionists. Special newspapers, pamphlets, speeches and slogans proclaimed the perfidious nature of European imperialism and nationalist leaders were expected to participate in this mass denunciation. While this campaign probably did help to break down some old loyalties, there were also complaints in Burma and the Philippines, colonies well on their way to independence, that the propaganda was too blatant; and the Japanese claims became less credible as the war progressed and conditions in the area were visibly deteriorating. As economic conditions worsened and actions by Japanese troops against civilians gave rise to resentment and criticism, the Greater East Asian Co-Prosperity Sphere appeared less desirable as a substitute for colonial government to many South-East Asians.

But it was the positive pro-nationalist propaganda which the Japanese emphasized somewhat later that probably developed the most lasting effect. The inauguration ceremonies of the nearly 'independent' states were widely publicized, as were the activities and speeches of the new leaders. Campaigns were instigated in praise of the past history and accom-

24 Sikh soldiers in Burma in 1945. Until the Second World War, most occupying Powers had preferred to use foreign troops within a colony; such forces were less likely to be influenced by urban nationalists.

plishments of the new nations, and flags, songs, plays, slogans and prose whipped up nationalist feelings within the population.

Some Japanese activities were distinctly detrimental to the development of national unity. Little was accomplished in the way of bringing into participation in national life the disparate peoples who lived outside the main population centres. In Burma Japanese suspicions of the loyalty of the hill peoples led them to acquiesce in precipitate nationalist actions against Christian groups. Stories of atrocities and forced conversions increased the bitterness of a people already pro-British and helped to light the fuse of the civil war which was to follow independence. In Malaya the mistreatment of the Chinese population fed both a growing sense of separate identity from the Malay majority and the dissident Communist movement. Out of the hatreds and dislocations of the war grew the Chinese dissatisfaction that led to the decade-long civil war in that country. In Indonesia the decision to give administrative control of the outer islands to the navy and Java and its environs to the army increased the sense of separate identity which had already been fostered by the Dutch policy of indirect and direct rule in approximately the same geographical areas. Thus Japanese policy in these three countries only exacerbated the elements of disunity found in the old colonial system.

This leads us to the third basic effect of the wartime occupation, the weakening of the old monopoly of modern weapons held by the colonial powers. Prior to the war the efforts of nationalists to mount attacks against European forces were inevitably doomed to defeat. Minor inter-war insurrections, such as the Saya San Rebellion in Burma, the 'Red Terror' in Indo-China and the 1926–27 revolts in the Indies, were put down with comparative ease by the far better trained and armed colonial forces. In most colonies the military forces had as their backbone foreign troops supplemented by recruits from minority ethnic groups from areas outside the main population centres. Thus the British maintained no Burman units for most of the inter-war years, preferring to depend upon battalions from hill tribes such as the Chins, Karens and Kachins, plus Indian professionals. A sizable percentage of the indigenous recruits in the East Indies were from Christian areas in the outer islands. Only in the Philippines was there a large national military force, which justified American confidence in it by fighting bravely against the Japanese advance. Usually the colonial powers felt it safer to draw their armed forces from areas and groups outside the influence of the urban nationalists. There were very few Burman, Javanese or Vietnamese officers in 1940 and almost no arms were available to nationalists who wanted to become involved in insurgent activity. The war ended that.

The Japanese actively sought to recruit and train military units in the former colonies. In some cases they employed men from the colonial forces, but to a great extent the new armies were composed of non-professionals – men with nationalist ideologies recruited from youth groups, universities and political organizations. This process was not totally successful, as there was often competition among military units and the instilling of professionalism into politically oriented individuals posed problems. For their part the South-East Asians complained about Japanese foot-dragging in building local forces, about excessive imperial control and about inferior weapons. Yet by the end of the war there existed large stockpiles of weapons for those who would later take up arms against the returning colonial powers and the independent governments that succeeded them. Generally, these military supplies came from four sources. First, the Japanese supplied units they considered loyal with arms as well as training. For their part the Allies did the same thing, providing arms to Chin, Karen and Kachin

25 This poster issued by the Netherlands government in 1944 depicted Japan as an octopus, its tentacles extended to embrace the whole of South-East Asia.

supporters in Burma, 'Free Thai' elements in Thailand, and, through the American OSS, to units under Ho Chi Minh in Indo-China. Thirdly, the invasions and counter-invasions of Burma and the Philippines allowed a leakage of weapons to those who wanted them. Finally, after their defeat the Japanese often voluntarily allowed nationalists to 'capture' arms from them, and Allied measures for the surrender of imperial troops were not always careful enough about accounting for weapons. There are stories of Japanese soldiers being ordered to drop their rifles and step forward, only to have Indonesians come up behind them and carry off their weapons. There is no way of assessing just how many rifles, pistols, rounds of ammunition, grenades, etc. fell into the hands of South-East Asians, but civil wars in Burma, Malaya, Indo-China, the Philippines and Indonesia were initially largely carried on with supplies obtained in the Second World War. No longer could the colonial powers be sure of defeating the now armed and trained nationalists.

What then was changed in South-East Asia by the events of the war? First and foremost, the whole colonial administrative, economic and social structure was disrupted, and disrupted fatally. The European could no longer lay claim to unquestioned authority over the area as he had previously done. He had been humiliatingly defeated in war, compelled to undertake forced-labour projects and driven into camps, and all of this by another Asian. When he returned from the prison camps or from Australia or India, or wherever he had fled, he came face to face with a society distinctly different from that which had existed less than four years earlier. The people had enjoyed a taste of independence, only symbolic perhaps, but they had seen their own leaders proclaimed president or premier, dealt with Asian rather than European administrators at all levels, been subjected to intensive anti-colonial and pro-nationalist propaganda, and had acquired arms and the training with which to challenge the returning colonialists. In sum, a significantly larger number of South-East Asians were (1) armed and trained for combat, (2) experienced in administration and politics, (3) ideologically committed to independence, (4) unwilling to accept the old social order, (5) more organized for political activity and (6) less respectful of colonial power. It should be emphasized that this change did not overtake all of South-East Asia. Many of the indigenous population still remained basically apolitical, wedded to their villages and families and unconcerned with politics and the establishment of national governments. Yet for most of the region the wartime period was a watershed, a fact that would become apparent in the crucial years that followed.

3 The Crucial Years

The break from traditional colonial patterns brought about by the Japanese interregnum was soon made apparent to the returning Europeans. They found fully fledged nationalist movements with their own governments, leaders and symbols. In Burma, Indonesia and Indo-China the main stream of nationalist opinion was prepared to fight for independence and trained military units were available to the nationalists.

In many ways the manner in which the metropolitan powers attempted to deal with post-war nationalism reflected their pre-war philosophies. Not that nothing had been learned from the war with Japan, but the shift in their attitudes and approach was insufficient to meet the almost revolutionary changes that they now faced. Their reactions varied considerably across the region but can be considered on three levels: acceptance of the reality of independence, rejection of total freedom for their colonies in spite of the existence of strong nationalist movements, and support of the *status quo* in the light of political apathy within the population. It would be delightfully simple to state that the particular reaction of each colonial power was closely correlated with post-war political activities within South-East Asia, but the situation was far too complex for this.

In the cases of the Philippines and Burma the road to independence was comparatively easy. The Americans lived up to their pre-war promise, although with some hesitation in view of the devastation wrought by the war and the difficulties the new Filipino republic would consequently face. However, the old leadership was restored, the military government dismantled and independence declared on 4 July 1946. The agreement to free the country, fulfilment of MacArthur's pledge to return to the islands and heavy American aid all combined to ease relations with the former colonial ruler. Although Filipino nationalism was to give rise to increased antagonisms in later years, the first post-war decade was basically one of amity.

For Burma independence was not so automatic, and it was not until 4 January 1948 that the British formally handed over sovereignty. Among the factors which aided Burmese efforts to gain their freedom were the change of sides by the nationalist army which supported the British in the final stages of the war, the existence of a strong national political organization, the AFPFL, good leadership under General Aung San, and the effect of British agreements to grant independence to India, Pakistan and Ceylon. Nevertheless immediate independence for Burma was inhibited by other factors. Burma had suffered severely from a war which had twice been fought across the country, destroying communications, devastating the economy and disrupting the administrative system. Most of the river transport, rail stock and docks were lost. At the beginning of the war many

26 The first Philippine president, Manuel L. Quezon, taking the oath after the formal establishment of commonwealth government, 1935. Detail of a mural in Manila City Hall.

27 Filipino patriot reporting during the Japanese occupation to a member of the American armed forces on the islands. Relatively amicable relations between local leaders and the United States hastened the approach of Philippine independence.

of the Indian merchants and professionals had fled, leaving a badly disturbed economy which was further damaged by scorched-earth policies, a loss of markets and the increase of squatters on agricultural land. The war had also seen civil servants flee to India, while others who remained in Burma had refused to co-operate with the nationalists. A second major reason for delay resulted from the fears of the hill peoples, who were not enamoured of the idea of domination by the majority, that an independent Burma would not recognize their rights. Finally, the political situation during the first post-war years was far from stable. Gone from power were the old political leaders of the 1930s, along with the wartime ruler Dr Ba Maw. The young men who controlled the AFPFL were of varying political hues and were in conflict both with the far left and with the older politicians.

Ultimately perhaps the greatest political tragedy was the assassination of Aung San and a number of key ministers in 1947. In spite of these difficulties, however, and despite some initial foot-dragging, the British agreed to full independence in 1947 and when it was formally granted the next year Burma took the opportunity to leave the Commonwealth. Because of the basic problems noted above, however, freedom was accompanied by decades of civil strife and economic stagnation.

If the United States and the United Kingdom were prepared to meet the nationalists with independence, the Dutch and French were ready to meet them primarily with force. The long conflicts and negotiations over the future of Indonesia and Indo-China were too complex to be described here. Instead, an effort will be made to note major similarities and differences between the experiences of the two countries, and to analyse the impact of the conflicts with the colonial powers on later political activities and attitudes. Six similarities between the two situations are apparent.

Defeated and occupied in war and humiliated in their colonies by the Japanese, neither France nor Holland was prepared to surrender its colonial territories without a struggle. Agreement was made more difficult by the character of the Indonesian and Vietnamese nationalist leadership. Sukarno was damned by the Dutch as a former puppet of the Japanese, a collaborationist and a man with strong Marxist tendencies. Ho Chi Minh was viewed as a Communist agent by the French, although at the time there was considerable speculation as to his true political views. Moreover, the attitudes prevalent in post-war Holland and post-war France were not conducive to compromise with the new South-East Asian leadership.

Secondly, the immediate post-war years saw political division within the governments of the metropolitan powers and between the leadership at home and their representatives in the colonies. In Holland there was little continuous, unified policy among the parties controlling the Dutch Parliament, while in the first post-war years the tripartite French Cabinet was composed of Catholic, Socialist and Communist members. Given these internal divisions it was difficult for the home governments to present clear and forceful positions in their negotiations with the nationalists. In addition, there were major policy disputes with their supposed agents in the colonies. The Dutch Acting Governor-General, H. Van Mook, was in continuous conflict with more conservative politicians at home, while anti-nationalist officials in Indo-China more than once attempted to sabotage negotiations with the Viet Minh. Both problems probably helped to initiate and then to extend the colonial wars that developed.

28 Aung San, the
'father of independent
Burma', on a visit to
London in the 1940s.

There were also divisions and conflicts within the nationalist movements of both colonies. In Indonesia, areas outside Java were less attracted to nationalism and the Dutch were able to play upon traditional regional and religious animosities. In Java itself more moderate Indonesian negotiators were under constant pressure from radical nationalists unwilling to accept compromise. The same regional and political divisions existed in Vietnam, where the rivalry between Communist and anti-Communist groups for leadership of the independence movement was so virulent that an external observer might well have wondered whether the defeat of one wing by the other was not regarded as more important than the fight against the French. In any case, with both the colonial and the nationalist forces divided, the chances for successful negotiation towards independence were minimized.

These difficulties in reaching a negotiated settlement largely explain a fourth similarity between the situations in Indo-China and Indonesia: in both recourse was had to overt, large-scale force in order to bring the nationalist movement under control. In Indonesia the Dutch carried out two 'police actions' in 1947 and 1948, which enabled them to capture most of the nationalist leadership and gave them temporary control of the archipelago. Nevertheless, loss of life in this conflict was considerably less than in the eight-year war between the French and the Viet Minh. In Indo-China, fighting was more extensive and more local nationals fought on the side of the colonial power. In both cases the efforts of the Europeans to reimpose their rule led to bitter reactions among the nationalists, further devastation of the economies of the metropolitan and colonial countries, the weakening of moderate forces and the distribution of still more arms to an increasingly politicized population.

These nationalist conflicts brought both Indonesia and Vietnam into the international arena to a greater degree than other South-East Asian states. Both became involved in the 'cold war' as the combatants sought support for their positions and foreign powers sought to influence the negotiations to their own advantage. The Indonesian situation was constantly before the United Nations from 1946 to 1950 and UN good offices were used in both 'police actions'. The Soviet Union and the Afro-Asian states argued that the UN had a positive role to play in colonial affairs in supporting independence movements, and they sought Dutch withdrawal; meanwhile the older Dutch, French and British colonial powers claimed that the conflicts were a domestic matter which should be left to the Netherlands and the Indonesians to decide between themselves. The United States, caught between its traditional anti-colonial stand and its new role as a world power and a protagonist in the 'cold war', attempted to mediate. Ultimately it was through international and primarily US pressure on the Dutch that a settlement was reached. Without such pressure Indonesian independence would certainly have been delayed indefinitely.

In Indo-China the French, Vietnamese and Cambodians all sought international support, and their representatives launched public relations campaigns to win foreign approval. While the conflicts that developed remained largely outside the United Nations, the actions of the United States and the Soviet Union were increasingly influential as the former gave support to anti-Communist forces in South Vietnam and the latter put pressure on the Viet Minh to accept the 1954 Geneva accords. In the first years of the struggle, however, it was the Nationalist Chinese who were important, vacillating between aiding and hindering the cause of Vietnamese independence. They also occupied northern Indo-China at the end of the war, thus denying the French control over this important centre of nationalist activity. In one of those delicious ironies of history the Chinese refused to relinquish the territory until the French agreed to end the unequal treaties they had obtained through occupation of Chinese land in the previous century. Finally, the victory of the Communist Chinese in 1947 put a pro-nationalist power right on the border of Indo-China, further endangering the French presence. In sum, while the UN was absent, the actions of the world powers were crucial to the type of settlement finally reached.

As a footnote it should be added that both the French and Dutch were well aware of events in one another's colonies and in at least one case a Dutch emissary was sent to Indo-China to study French policies.

A final similarity was to be seen in the 'settlement' of the conflicts, the Round Table Conference between the Dutch and Indonesians at The Hague in 1949 and the 1954 Geneva accords which ended French colonial rule in Indo-China. The two agreements were quite different in type, the first being a bilateral settlement between the two protagonists whereas the Geneva negotiations resulted in a series of declarations by the interested powers (except for the government in Saigon and the American administration in Washington, the former of which was not invited and the latter of which refused to sign). Both accords, however, reflected the heterogeneity of the two colonies and the divisions among the nationalists. Indo-China had already seen the splitting-off of independent Cambodia and Laos the year prior to the Geneva conference, and the 1954 agreements drew a temporary armistice line in Vietnam at the 17th parallel. In Indonesia the Round Table Conference brought about the transitory establishment of a federal system in the archipelago with a series of semi-autonomous states, and considerable separatist sentiment in those outer islands where nationalism had never been strong. The federal system lasted less than a year, since the leadership of the central government set out to destroy what it believed to be a Dutch plot to divide and rule the new nation. In Indo-China, on the other hand, the 'temporary' division quickly became established. The reasons for the different outcomes are not difficult to ascertain. The Indonesian government was not under international pressure to remain federal in structure and the local separatists were militarily weak, although regional guerrilla activities continued for another decade. In Indo-China, Laos and Cambodia were states with independent histories of their own, distinguishing them from the rest of the former French colony, and their sovereignty was internationally guaranteed. At the same time the southern half of Vietnam was able to assert an independent role not only because it contained major groups antagonistic towards the government in the North, but also, and far more important, because it had a strong military ally in the United States. The point to be noted in both cases is that initial boundaries established in the Hague and Geneva accords reflected more than artificial colonial divisions, but the question of the ultimate unification of the states concerned was primarily related to international and military considerations.

The Indonesian and Indo-Chinese cases also display some obvious points of difference. One was led by a local nationalist leadership largely Socialist in character while the other was under Communist control. Fighting was more intense and of longer duration in Indo-China. Dutch offers during negotiations were basically more generous than those of the French. There was no single major nationalist organization such as the Viet Minh in Indonesia. Yet all these differences, as well as the previously mentioned similarities, would appear to be dominated by the single fact that neither the Dutch nor the French were initially prepared to recognize the demands

29 The American commander in Vietnam, General William C. Westmoreland, takes the salute with Air Vice-Marshal Ky, 1968. South Vietnam's dependence on America increased dramatically as the war escalated in the late 1950s and 1960s.

of the nationalists for independence and both were ultimately ready to fight rather than to negotiate. What South-East Asia would be like today if they had followed the patterns set in the Philippines and Burma can only be a matter of conjecture.

The final type of colonial reaction to post-war nationalist activity was one of retaining the basic *status quo* in the light of general political apathy. In both Malaya and Laos there was little apparent nationalist sentiment in 1945 among the majority of the population. In Malaya the war years had seen political activity primarily among members of the Chinese and Indian communities. Poorly treated by the Japanese, many Chinese were attracted to the Communists, and guerrilla activity was initiated with British help. Only a minority of the Chinese were involved, however, and the Malayan People's Anti-Japanese Army, the core of guerrilla strength, numbered only about seven thousand men at its height. The Japanese attempted to rally the Indians against British colonial rule, but propaganda and recruiting were directed more towards independence for India than towards freedom in Malaya. During the occupation the Malay nationalist movement was almost dormant, with the exception of a small left-wing group. Even symbolic independence was not granted the colony by the Japanese.

Thus when the war ended Malaya had developed neither a national leadership nor a mass organization against the returning British administration. Chinese Communist elements were opposed to the re-establishment of British rule, but the Malay majority was suspicious of Chinese chauvinism and the traditional Malay leadership was not attracted to the Communist ideology and goals. When the Communists began their decade-long insurrection against the British in 1948 their membership was almost entirely Chinese, and this fact further exacerbated Sino-Malay relations since the Malays feared a victory of both the Chinese and Communism. The combination of historic divisions within Malaya, low pre-war and wartime political activity, traditional leadership and racial antipathies all helped to dampen demands for immediate independence. It was not until the Communists were defeated and the Malays had developed better political organization and leadership that independence was granted in 1956.

Laos was quite a different situation. Here French inaction reflected a lack of nationalist concern throughout the population that was, initially, almost total. During the war most of the developed sections of the country had come under Thai suzerainty and political activity was minimal. Following the war a French-controlled government was formed, although a lack of political awareness and the persistence of traditional feudal divisions meant

that the colony was not yet a nation. Most Lao and almost all the hill tribes remained outside the national political culture, and the small size of the urban centres (none had a population over twenty-five thousand in 1945) hampered the introduction of modern organizational methods. Not until 1950 was the pro-Communist Pathet Lao formed to fight the French, and in general nationalist politics were more concerned with personal intrigue than with the development of effective organizations. Under these conditions the French were not quick to offer democratic reforms and when independence came in 1953 it was not primarily due to indigenous nationalist pressure.

THE CONTINUING IMPACT OF THE NATIONALIST MOVEMENTS

The long-range effects of these crucial post-war years on later South-East Asian society will be discussed in later chapters. What was their short-term impact? Six fundamental consequences can be observed during the next decade, although their influence was not uniform throughout the whole region and they were not necessarily related either to the type of colonial régime, the extent of violence during the struggle for independence or the economic and social levels of the society involved.

30 Civil war in Burma, April 1949. Government troops resting before a confrontation with the rebel forces.

31 Civil strife aggravated the damage caused by the war and seriously impeded rehabilitation. At one period naval patrol boats were used on the Irrawaddy to protect valuable cargoes from attack by guerrillas.

Of central importance in explaining political change in post-war South-East Asia is the varied impact of the destruction wrought by the combination of the Second World War and the colonial conflicts that followed. Where devastation was of a relatively low order the state was able to get back to its pre-war level of production and to avoid much of the mass dissatisfaction stemming from unmet needs. It is noteworthy that the states where this happened include the only democracies in the region today, none of which developed strong anti-colonial mass ideologies. Both Malaya and Thailand experienced comparatively low levels of wartime destruction and no major violence in the first few years after the war. Both were able to return to pre-war levels of output by 1947–48.[1] The Philippines, which had been badly damaged during the war, particularly around Manila, was not the scene of colonial war and received heavy American rehabilitation support. The islands returned to their aggregate pre-war production in 1947 and *per capita* output in 1950. Both Malaya and the Philippines experienced Communist-led insurrections after 1948 but were able to maintain growth.

For other states, and particularly Burma, Indonesia and Vietnam, the destruction wrought in the 1940s had profound effects on the next generation. Burma was not only badly hurt by the war against the Japanese, but the post-war period was unsettled and within two years of 1945, before independence was launched, a generation-long civil war began. This combination of circumstances made a complete rehabilitation of the country impossible. Aggregate pre-war production was not attained until 1957 and an equivalent *per capita* output has probably yet to be reached. The reconstruction of the damage to communications, factories and agricultural production caused by the war was hindered and often completely halted by post-war violence. Valuable mines were only sporadically reopened, river-boats were attacked by rebels, and farmers were afraid to grow their crops. As one example of the problem, for a decade after 1948 passenger trains could not be run at night between Rangoon and Mandalay for fear of attack. Furthermore the effort to establish a common national identity and to transform the former colony into a nation state came into conflict with the local nationalist aspirations of the Shans, Karens, Kachins and other hill groups.

The problems in Indonesia were almost as serious. The Japanese interregnum did not bring so much damage to property here, in spite of scorched-earth policies, but European economic activities were severely dislocated by the war. Perhaps more damaging over time were the short- and long-run effects of the nationalist movement. Western enterprises were unable to re-establish pre-war production, particularly in the areas where there had been fighting. However, the destruction caused by the earlier scorched-earth policies and the deterioration of the wartime period, combined with delays in rehabilitation resulting from the post-war colonial wars, could probably have been reversed had it not been for the bitterness generated between the Dutch and the Indonesians in the post-war years. Indonesian nationalists were not prepared to allow their former colonial masters to return to their old privileged positions and foreign enterprise was slow to re-develop. It was thus not until 1953 that the islands once again attained the aggregate level of pre-war production and it was four years more before pre-war *per capita* output was reached. Within a year, however, civil war broke out between rebels in the outer islands and the government in Java, and Dutch nationals were evicted from the country with the result that the economy probably once again declined below its pre-war level. Thus in Indonesia the war for independence and the attitudes it spawned were crucial in delaying economic recovery.

While statistical evidence for Indo-China is even more limited than for elsewhere, it would appear that the conflict between the Vietnamese nationalists and the French meant that it was not until 1954 that re-habilitation of the country could fully begin. This was not so much restoration of damage wrought by the Second World War, since there had been comparatively little fighting and the Japanese held complete control of the colony for only six months in 1945. Far more damaging had been the long colonial war that followed, which brought widespread shifts in the population, delayed necessary improvements of factories and plantations, and took working-age males out of the economy. It is an open question whether either North or South Vietnam got back to the pre-war level of production prior to the renewal of fighting in 1958–59.

The efforts to obtain independence and to create a nation thus either helped to provide the foundation for stable political development or else hindered it by placing a further burden of rehabilitation on leaders who were attempting both to make good the damage inflicted during the Japanese period and to form a new polity.

A second short-term consequence of the post-war years in South-East Asia was that the conflicts generated by the unwillingness of the European powers to accept the demand for independence diminished the existing pool of trained administrative personnel while at the same time it forced others to develop new administrative capacity. Colonial wars compelled some South-East Asians to learn military trades quickly while others were receiving 'on-the-job training' in running new governments. Though some had served under the Japanese, these were the first independent commands for many of the later military and civil leaders of the region. However, the bitterness surrounding some of these colonial conflicts also resulted in a severe drain on the limited trained manpower. Of course, European administrators lost their places with the coming of independence, except for a relatively small number of expatriates hired until nationals could take their positions. But the acceleration of 'Asianization' under the pressure of nationalism brought a speedy end to the role of the expatriates in most administrations by the end of the first decade after independence, and much sooner in North Vietnam and Burma. Perhaps more serious was the loss that resulted from the estrangement of indigenous civil servants and military personnel. This was particularly true of members of ethnic or religious minorities who had sympathized with the old colonial régime and were dissatisfied with the new independent government. In Burma senior civil servants who had fled to India with the British, Indians formerly employed by the colonial administration and members of ethnic groups in rebellion against the Rangoon government found themselves demoted, forced to resign or in some cases driven to active rebellion. In Vietnam many professional and administrative personnel were among the hundreds of thousands of Catholics who fled south after the 1954 Geneva accords. In the South these new immigrants helped to fill positions lost by local people who joined the Viet Minh, went into exile overseas or were killed in the war with France. Indonesia was unwilling to accept those who had fought with the Dutch, while members of the military and the civil service who later joined anti-government insurgents were *personae non gratae* for many years. This was particularly true of missionary-trained Christians who had been employed by the Dutch in positions of civil and military trust. When there had been considerable 'Asianization' prior to independence and/or a smooth transition to self-government, it was easier to develop stable economic and political systems, as exemplified by the Philippines, Malaysia and Singapore.

Thirdly, as noted in the preceding section, the post-war struggles for independence exacerbated communal tensions throughout South-East Asia. Groups which had occupied protected or privileged positions in the colonial system were usually unprepared to accept what they regarded as the domination of new nationalist elements of a different communal composition. Examples of this type of conflict generated by the new patterns of power are numerous. In Burma the Christian-led Karens had long tended to be pro-British and during the war had found themselves targets of abuse by over-zealous Buddhist Burman nationalists. Karen demands for autonomy or even independence after the war were resisted and ultimately resulted in civil war. In Malaya we have already mentioned the tension which developed between left-wing elements of the Chinese community who desired the elimination of British rule and the Malays who maintained a more evolutionary and apolitical stance. Vietnam experienced a similar type of hostility between the Catholic minority and the Viet Minh and by the time of the Geneva accords of 1954 most Christians in northern Vietnam saw the only solution for themselves to be exile in the South. In Indonesia Christian and other communal groups in the outer islands feared domination by the Javanese in the new Republic, and considerable unrest followed independence.

To a great extent these violent outbreaks of inter-communal antagonism were an outgrowth of the failure – or deliberate refusal – of the colonial régimes to foster a sense of common nationality in the pre-war years. By granting special privileges to Christians, maintaining the privileged position of local rulers under the system of indirect rule, refusing in some colonies at least to countenance nation-wide political activity and limiting educational opportunities, the colonial administrations preserved a sense of separatism and generated inter-group rivalry. In turn the nationalists who came into power after the war were slow to recognize legitimate differences and the fears of minority groups. The result was communal civil war in one form or another in almost every new state in the region.

Another short-term effect of the crucial post-war years was that the bitter conflicts involved in the struggle for independence generated strong anti-colonial and anti-capitalist attitudes within the new ruling élites of Indonesia, Indo-China and Burma. Sukarno insisted that Indonesian society would never be completely free until imperialism and capitalism were totally destroyed, including all vestiges of political, economic and cultural 'neo-colonialism', defined as Western political interference, foreign investment and 'decadent' customs.[2] The leadership of the Viet Minh accepted the fundamental ideological tenets of Marxism-Leninism, which considered both capitalism and imperialism to be incompatible with true independence. U Nu of Burma argued that it was 'impossible to view the two in isolation' and strongly supported his own brand of Socialism.[3] As we shall see in the next chapter, these attitudes were in part the outcome of pre-war intellectual influences derived from European Marxist thought. However, the emotional anti-Westernism proclaimed in later years by many nationalists was also nurtured by events and by experience of foreign duplicity.

The Japanese had helped to spread anti-Western propaganda and to inculcate national pride. The formation of 'puppet' governments within the Co-Prosperity Sphere provided the peoples of South-East Asia with the symbolic paraphernalia of the nation state. The first post-war years were even more critical in increasing bitterness towards the metropolitan powers. The long colonial wars in Indo-China and Indonesia were bound to exacerbate the attitude of South-East Asians towards the powers which resorted to force to maintain their hold over their former colonial territories. The capture of most of the Indonesian leadership during the second Dutch 'police action' was not exactly conducive to future cordial relations. Of equal importance in all probability was the feeling that the European powers were working with anti-nationalist indigenous groups to sabotage independence and national unity. In Burma there was a common presumption among the nationalists that Karen and other dissidents were receiving both sympathy and arms from British supporters. During the colonial conflict Indonesian spokesmen accused the Dutch of establishing puppet states friendly to the Netherlands and of fostering anti-Javanese attitudes on the outer islands. Certainly there is indisputable evidence that the Dutch worked vigorously to counteract nationalist sentiment in regions under their control and lent political and military support to elements opposed to the forces of Sukarno. In Vietnam prior to the Geneva agreements the nationalists legitimately condemned the French for attempting to foster anti-Viet Minh political leadership, and after 1954 the North Vietnamese felt cheated of the fruits of victory by American support of the régime of Ngo Dinh Diem in the South. Nationalist leaders in all three states firmly believed that colonial intransigence towards independence and/or support for internal dissidents were closely tied to capitalist economic interests in the area. Capitalism and imperialism being considered two sides of the same coin, post-independence attitudes tended to be suspicious of foreign economic interests, which Sukarno, like Nkrumah in Africa, described as neo-colonialism. In sum, the bitterness generated by European efforts to counter nationalism in the 1940s was to form the foundation for the ideologies of many South-East Asian states in the following decade.

The character of the nationalist movement and European reactions to it also affected the particular character of the institutional arrangements accepted by the new states. Two examples are worth commenting upon, federalism in Indonesia and the constitutional government of the Philippines. The fact that Indonesia is a widespread archipelago with considerable linguistic and ethnic heterogeneity would appear to recommend a federal system as the ideal institutional arrangement. Federalism, it can be argued, would best reflect the diversity of the islands and would respect traditional local politics. However, as part of their effort to counter nationalism the Dutch established fifteen federal units in the first years after the Japanese occupation. Most of these were little more than puppets of the colonial administration, although in the case of East Indonesia, the oldest federal state, there appeared to be both considerable indigenous support and local autonomy. As previously noted, the federal system was incorporated into the final agreement between the Dutch and the Indonesian nationalists at The Hague, but within a year a unitary state was formed with minimal violence. Since that time proposals for re-establishing a federal state have been effectively resisted on the basis of its colonial associations and even supporters have admitted that if a federal system were to be formed it would have to be called by a different name.

The pattern in the Philippines was different in so far as the peaceful achievement of independence under American auspices led to the acceptance of a constitutional system modelled after that of the colonial power. As we shall see in Chapter 5 the Filipino nationalists copied the presidential and congressional institutions of the United States (the only country in South-East Asia to do so), together with the party system, judicial review, and even such niceties as the item veto, a method recommended by many American reformers to veto specific items in a Bill. More important, the evolutionary character of the nationalist movement in the Philippines ensured that these institutions enjoyed more than a symbolic role.

The sixth and final consequence of the crucial post-war period concerns the international repercussions of the nationalist movements in South-East Asia. These are difficult to calculate in any precise fashion. However, we can note several general developments that rose out of the situation. Most important of all, the achievement of independence in South and South-East Asia gave a strong impetus to efforts to eliminate colonialism in other parts of the world. The new Asian states were the first non-white-controlled territories, except for the mandated states of the Middle East, to which any European power gave independence in the twentieth century. The British had granted Commonwealth status to white Dominions such as Australia and Canada and complete independence to the Republic of Ireland. Indonesia and the Philippines were the only major colonies of the Dutch and Americans, who had not granted freedom to other smaller island territories. The French refused independence to any land under the *tricolor*, with the exception of mandates in the Middle East and Haiti in 1804. Thus, the granting of freedom to the new states of South and South-East Asia was a major break in policy which had immediate repercussions elsewhere. Both African nationalists and European administrators and policy-makers learned lessons from these first new nations, and there is little doubt that independence for African colonies was hastened by the achievements and tensions experienced in Asia.

Secondly, the conflicts in South-East Asia, particularly those in Indonesia and Indo-China, brought new international forces into the region. Except for the Philippines, South-East Asia had primarily been a Western European preserve. With the involvement of the United Nations and the merging of local issues in the cold war, it became impossible for the metropolitan powers to treat colonial questions as though they were simply domestic issues. South-East Asia was no longer an exotic, unknown backwater – it had entered the world political arena.

At the same time the issues raised by the nationalist movements in the post-war years led other countries to reconsider their basic policies regarding colonialism. The United States, which had never considered itself a colonial power, and had, in fact, prided itself on being a defender of dependent peoples, was compelled by reason of its cold war policies to support the Dutch, French and British imperialists. The Australians, shaken out of their isolation by the Second World War and perceiving that events in South-East Asia were intimately linked with their own future, broke with the British and supported the Indonesians against the Dutch. Newly independent India viewed conflicts in the area as a result of the machinations of the white powers and emerged as a major defender of the oppressed Asian peoples.

In sum, the states of South-East Asia at the end of the independence struggle were all, at various levels, confronted by problems arising from their new experiments in nation-building. All faced difficulties with communalism; all had to cope with economies based upon agricultural and extractive products; and all were ruled by a new leadership. Some were luckier or better prepared than others, but the majority found themselves faced with three central problems. First, the destruction and deterioration resulting from the Second World War and the post-war conflicts left them with a major task of rehabilitation. Secondly, Indo-China, Burma and Indonesia were each involved in what was to prove a lengthy civil war. In the first two the bloodletting lasted more than a generation, while in Indonesia communal and regional violence was to erupt sporadically for more than a decade. Finally, poor preparation by the colonial powers meant a paucity of trained technical personnel and experienced political leadership.

In the following chapters we shall look at South-East Asia in the early 1970s, attempting to judge what remains of the colonial-nationalist legacy and using as our frame of reference the ideologies, institutions and social patterns formed in the colonial period, changed by the Japanese occupation and reformed by the post-war nationalist movement.

32 South Vietnamese soldier, a symbol of the bitter fighting that has dogged his country for a generation.

4 The Ideological Legacy

While European and American commentators were debating the end of ideology, South-East Asia was a cockpit of ideological conflict. Various forms of Socialism, democracy and nationalism were being presented by both national leaders and their opponents. In this chapter we shall attempt to analyse what happened to the ideologies that developed out of the interaction between the colonial and nationalist heritages, assessing the changes that have taken place and why. We shall take as our basis the ideologies current in the 1940s, particularly democracy, Socialism and nationalism, each of which has claimed its advocates for over half a century but each of which in the process of time has diverged considerably from its original content.

Most of the new leaders of South-East Asia inherited an attachment to Western democratic values, although in some cases their attitudes were influenced by Communist or native thinking that challenged orthodox democratic ideals. Political spokesmen in the Philippines, Malaysia and Burma in particular strongly supported undiluted Western democratic values. Filipino politicians from the major parties recognized the legacy of American ideals and proclaimed their advocacy of competitive politics and basic human rights. The nation's constitution reflected Jeffersonian principles, and the institutions formed were arranged so as to protect individual rights. At least theoretically Philippine democratic ideology as publicly expressed at the time of independence was largely an extension of American political values.

Burma might have entered into independence with an ideological position less democratic in a Western sense if it had not been for the death of Aung San. The 'Father' of independent Burma was not totally enamoured of liberal democracy and more than once expressed his personal belief that a new nation state needed strong leadership. Democracy needed to be tempered by the immediate needs of the state. However, with the arrival in power of U Nu, there came into office a man publicly dedicated to basic democratic principles. He continued to express these views even when the military came into power in 1958 and carefully defined his standpoint when he was returned to office with an overwhelming mandate in 1960. 'Democracy', he stated,

> may be broadly described as freedom to do as one pleases subject to the legitimate rights and interest of others. In other words, it involves self-restraint, tolerance, and forbearance, three virtues with which, unfortunately, human nature is not richly endowed. . . . In practical terms, it means that a Government brought to power through a democratic path . . . must recognize that it is inherent in the democratic system that another party may be brought to power at the next election, and it must work to produce those conditions in which the transfer of power to the new Government may take place smoothly and peacefully. . . .[1]

Other national leaders also came forward in support of democratic values upon their assumption of power. Sihanouk of Cambodia proclaimed that he was attempting to establish a democratic polity. He denied that Communism could be described as democratic and stated that the 'authentic' democracy he was forming was much like that of France or Italy.[2] In Cambodia it was admitted that democracy was as yet not perfectly developed but the model being copied was Western in character. Tengku Abdul Rahman and other leaders of Malayan independence did not stray from the pattern of British parliamentary democracy. Part II of the federal constitution guaranteed essential political liberties and the institutions were developed in line with Western European models. Even in Thailand the period immediately following the war displayed a major effort to emulate democratic systems and the 1946 constitution attempted to institutionalize their precepts. The short-lived post-war government of Pridi Phanomyang was certainly Social Democratic in temper although powerful elements in Thai politics were not of like mind.

A somewhat more diluted type of liberal democracy was present elsewhere. Indonesia was an interesting case in point. At the end of the war the nationalists expected the Americans to take over from the Japanese, and when the British arrived instead they found trams and walls decorated with quotations from the United States Declaration of Independence and Abraham Lincoln's speeches. In addition, there were numerous spokesmen for Western ideals who supported evolutionary Social Democracy. However, it was President Sukarno who was to become the chief spokesman for the Indonesian national ideology and at this time he was cautious

71

33 Thai monk with his traditional begging-bowl. Monks in Thailand have abjured
the major political roles played by their Burmese and Vietnamese counterparts.

about accepting all the tenets of liberal democracy. In his most famous early speech which proclaimed the Pantja Sila, or five principles to guide the country, he stated,

> And now what is the third principle? That principle is the principle of *mufakat*, unanimity, the principle of *perwakilan*, representation, the principle of *permusjarawatan*, deliberation amongst representatives.[3]

This was not the articulation of a European model, but was rather a reflection of what Sukarno believed to be the traditional village pattern. He later explained the meaning of these terms to the United Nations:

> The only way in which it can function satisfactorily is by means of unanimity arising out of deliberation. Or, to use the Indonesian terms, by *mufakat* arising from *musjawarah*. Deliberations should be held in such a way that there is no contest between opposing points of view, no resolutions and counter-resolutions, no taking of sides, but only a persistent effort to find common ground in solving a problem. From such deliberation there arises a consensus, a unanimity, which is more powerful than a resolution forced through by a majority of votes, a resolution perhaps not accepted, or perhaps resented, by the minority.[4]

Thus Indonesia in the first years of independence was the scene of a welter of definitions of democracy, though Sukarno was increasingly in the forefront as spokesman for the national ideology.

Socialism in one form or another was a central theme in the ideologies of the early post-war leadership of Indonesia, Burma, Vietnam, Singapore and Thailand. It was also espoused by minority parties in Malaysia and the Philippines. As previously noted, nationalists in the region tended to equate capitalism with imperialism and support for Socialism was to a considerable degree the outgrowth of experience with colonial régimes. Not only did the politically aware feel at the mercy of colonial commercial interests, but, ironically, many were drawn to Socialist principles by Western writers and activists. At the same time, there existed no universal definition of Socialism among its proponents. Evolutionary Socialism, 'Trotskyism', 'orthodox' Communism and indigenous beliefs were all prevalent during this period, although democratic Socialism and Marxism-Leninism were most prominent.

Ideological spokesmen for Burma, Indonesia and Thailand all supported various forms of democratic evolutionary Socialism. U Nu of Burma had become fascinated with Fabian Socialism and Marxism as a young man, at which time he proclaimed: 'We are out to crush that evil economic system whereby a handful of people hold a monopoly, while the masses of Burma remain in endless poverty.'[5] Upon his attainment of power he worked for a planned economy based upon an amalgamation of Western democratic and traditional Buddhist ideals. In his first years in office as prime minister he was both strongly anti-capitalist and anti-Communist, declaring that the only difference between the two was that whereas in the former 'a share of the profits goes to the capitalist owners – or shareholders – in a Communist country a similar or even larger share goes to the state.'[6] He also disagreed with the totalitarian and class war tenets of Communism, while the materialism of both it and capitalism was in contradiction to his Buddhist beliefs.

President Sukarno of Indonesia had been intimately involved in Socialist political and intellectual activities since the 1920s. The fourth principle in his Pantja Sila, while rejecting Western political democracy as insufficient, called for 'political-economic democracy', arguing that in the West people were 'at the mercy of the capitalist'. In the early years of his presidency, Sukarno defined Socialism in vague terms of social justice and anti-capitalism while Indonesian political parties were attempting to provide more specific guidelines to their beliefs. Religious Socialists rejected the Marxist-Leninist position on class war, collectivism and national revolution while asserting that their platform was based upon Islam, a mixed economy and liberal democracy. The Socialist Party also accepted these tenets, with the exception of the role of Islam. The Communist Party for its part was formed along traditional Marxist-Leninist lines with some influence from indigenous beliefs. It stood for national revolution, nationalization of major industry and foreign investment, and the leadership of the workers and peasants. Indonesia in the first post-war years was a kaleidoscope of ideas, with almost all the major political factions paying obeisance to Socialist principles.

While minority elements within the nationalist movements of South-East Asia were proclaiming the need to march under the banner of Marxism-Leninism, only in Vietnam was that ideology in the mainstream of political life. Even so, the early Viet Minh statements were extremely vague about the structure and philosophy of the post-independence state to be established. Ho Chi Minh portrayed himself as a nationalist and played down his Communist background. His real beliefs were expressed in statements such as that in 1924 when he declared that the peasant was 'crucified on the bayonet of capitalist civilization and on the cross of prostituted Christianity'[7] or his draft of the 1930 Communist Party programme which was anti-capitalist and anti-imperialist and in favour of nationalization, class war and independence. Nevertheless, Vietnam in the 1940s was not stridently Marxist-Leninist although its leadership was drawn from the Communists.

The third part of the ideological trinity, nationalism, was, as we have noted, closely identified with anti-capitalism and anti-colonialism. We have already described the character of the nationalist movements, now we are primarily concerned with the character of the ideology that was generated. In doing so we need to stress three elements that were initially at the forefront, anti-colonialism, national unity and non-aggression.

Obviously, early nationalism was principally concerned with the attainment of independence from colonial domination. It requires little analysis of the speeches and statements of the leadership of South-East Asia during the 1940s to perceive the central place of attacks on imperialism and colonialism. These varied in character from Sukarno's emotional proclamation of Indonesia Merdeka (independence), and U Nu's belief that independence was necessary to protect Burmese traditions, to the 1945 Vietnamese Declaration of Independence which quoted from the American Declaration of Independence and the French Declaration of the Rights of Man. The Vietnamese might accuse the French of drowning uprisings in 'rivers of blood', Sukarno might support his views on nationalism by liberal quotation from Sun Yat Sen, Otto Bauer and Ernest Renan, but almost all sought freedom from colonialism.

A second basic ingredient in early nationalist thought was the essential need for national unity. Given the heterogeneous nature of the new states and the regional and communal conflicts accompanying independence, the leadership was well aware of the need for unity across religious, ethnic, racial and regional divisions. In these first years national unity was far more important than economic development to the élites. U Nu explicitly regarded himself as Burma's Abraham Lincoln trying to hold the Union together; the Indonesian national motto became 'Unity in Diversity' and the central theme in Viet Minh statements was the common purpose of the people and the need for unified support to defeat the French.

Finally, nationalism in the 1940s sought domestic goals and did not foresee using ideology as a basis for expansion. On the contrary, the leadership looked to the ideals of Sun Yat Sen and Mazzini, claiming that national independence was the necessary prerequisite to international co-operation. One of the clearest presentations of this position was to be found in the Pantja Sila, where Sukarno declared:

The nationalism we advocate is not the nationalism of isolation, not chauvinism as blazoned by people in Europe who say 'Deutschland über Alles', who say that there is none so great as Germany, whose people, they say, are supermen, corn-haired and blue-eyed 'Aryans', whom they consider the greatest in the world, while other nations are worthless. Do not let us hold by such principles, gentlemen, do not let us say that the Indonesian nation is the most perfect and the noblest whilst we belittle other peoples. We must proceed towards the unity of the world, the brotherhood of the world.[8]

What has happened to this trinity of democracy, Socialism and nationalism is the major subject of this chapter. It should be emphasized that few sharply defined regional trends can be ascertained with regard to any of these ideological precepts. Change has occurred, often precipitately, but at the present time it is difficult to pinpoint many common features.

Any analysis of the place of Western democracy in South-East Asia must initially cope with the difficulties its proponents have faced since independence. Burma experimented with parliamentary democracy for a decade under U Nu, but internal party dissension, corruption, maladministration and civil war brought the military into power in 1958. After another short democratic interregnum the military again stepped in, this time to eradicate permanently any vestiges of liberal democracy. In Thailand efforts to foster liberal concepts have been short-lived, since brief attempts to establish civilian rule have been punctuated by long intervals of military control. Cambodia maintained a tenuous one-party democracy under Sihanouk which paid obeisance to liberal tenets. The 1970 *coup*, which had military support, ended that particular experiment, although the institutions remained. In South Vietnam there was some show for a short time of the external forms of democracy, but it was essentially window-dressing, and after the death of Ngo Dinh Diem the country passed under a series of military dictatorships. Under President Thieu the country is again experiencing highly personalized government which seeks to maintain the external symbols of democracy. Malaysia maintained a Western parliamentary model until the communal riots in 1969, after which it was suspended for two years. The country has now returned to the former pattern, but with added restrictions on dissent. Indonesia held free elections in the 1950s, but under Sukarno's 'Guided Democracy' the parliament was reorganized into functional groups, opposition parties were eliminated and civil rights were curtailed. With the end of Sukarno's rule

34 Parliament House, Kuala Lumpur, a majestic embodiment of post–independence Malaysia's desire to follow a form of the Western democratic system.

in the mid-1960s President Suharto and the military formed another highly restricted democratic system. Until 1972 the Philippines appeared to be the one lasting example of party politics in the region and one of those rare cases in Asia and Africa in which the opposition was allowed to come to power without a resultant *coup*. However, in 1972 President Marcos employed the military to 'reform' the country and put an at least temporary end to Western democracy in the archipelago. Only in Singapore has democracy remained relatively untouched since independence and even there a single party has dominated politics and radical opponents have been jailed. Of the two other states, Laos never did establish a working democratic polity and North Vietnam has made no pretence of accepting Western democratic concepts. The position by 1972, therefore, was that the military was in a dominant position in Burma, Thailand, Cambodia, South Vietnam, the Philippines and Indonesia, although it shared power with civilian elements in the majority of cases. Liberal democracy was alive and relatively well only in Malaysia and Singapore, though in both countries there were greater restrictions on the opposition than would be found in Western Europe. The remaining two countries were authoritarian or totalitarian. Given these changes, what happened to democratic ideology in South-East Asia?

Within those states whose leaders initially accepted much of the legacy of Western democracy we can find three major trends, the permanent rejection of liberal democracy, a temporary rejection due to 'unusual circumstances' and support for a somewhat restricted democratic system. The mainstream of the ideologies of Burma and Indonesia no longer accept liberal democracy as it is understood in the West. When the Burmese military came to power in 1962 under General Ne Win the national ideology became the 'Burmese Way to Socialism'.[9] The new concept was that parliamentary democracy contained 'too many loopholes for abuse to be of value to a country like Burma' and had failed in the country due to 'defects, weaknesses, and loopholes, its abuses and the absence of mature public opinion'. The key ideological document of the period, *The Burmese Way to Socialism*, argued that 'the nation's Socialist aims cannot be achieved with any assurance by means of the form of Parliamentary Democracy we have so far experienced'. In the following decade the military continued to reject liberal democracy as a desirable means of forming a Socialist state. Instead, a rather vague set of goals were fostered, defined in a mixture of traditional Burmese and modern Marxist terms. When democracy is established, the military argue that it will have to fit into the new economic

78

and political circumstances of the nation. There is no question that Burma's
new leadership has rejected the early post-colonial support for liberal
concepts. However, neither has it totally accepted the precepts of Western
Marxism-Leninism. Instead it has sought a uniquely Burmese solution to
the nation's problems. The exact nature of the final system has yet to be
delineated after a decade of army rule.

While Sukarno was less than enchanted by Western democracy in 1945,
other Indonesian politicians were strongly attracted to its precepts. Yet, as
Sukarno came to dominate the national ideology, his principles largely
became those of the country. Central to his philosophy in his last years was
an attack upon 'free-fight liberalism', '50 per cent plus 1 democracy' and
'majoracracy' as he argued that 'the idea of an opposition, whether loyal or
not, does not fit our traditional society or our traditional ideas'. By the
late 1950s, he no longer paid lip-service to such Western concepts and

35 Pre-independence election poster, Singapore. Democratic principles have remained comparatively undiluted since.

proposed instead 'Guided Democracy'. 'Yes, indeed,' he said, 'without concealing anything we have made a complete divorce from Western democracy, which is free-fight liberalism, but on the other hand since ancient times we have flatly rejected dictatorships.'[10] The new system denied the efficacy of, and, in fact, considered dangerous to the well-being of the state, such basic elements of Western democracy as party competition, individualism and organized criticism. 'Guided Democracy' remained a somewhat vague ideology based upon deliberation, unanimity and 'democracy with leadership'. The Indonesian people were to be represented by functional groups, but President Sukarno was to remain the supreme representative of the people's aspirations. Opponents argued that the President had established an ideology under whose guise Sukarno could secure dictatorial powers.

The military men who overthrew Sukarno had publicly supported the former President's ideological precepts when he was at his height. In their initial years of control there was considerable debate as to the form and ideology of the government they were forming. Although there was conflict over the role of parties and political competition, however, there was agreement that the new system must support the efforts of the régime to form a stable, anti-Communist polity. Ultimately an electoral system, political parties and limited parliamentary democracy were accepted within a framework that guaranteed the continued dominance of forces friendly to the military. Communists and their adherents were not allowed to participate and all candidates had to agree not

> to slander, show contempt or disrespect of the government or government officials, individuals, groups, organizations, or a foreign country, or to commit any other acts/activities contrary to the ethics/moral code of Pantja Sila Principles.

Of course, the military was the final authority in interpreting such rules. In essence, then, Indonesia now upholds another form of Guided Democracy.

Several states in the region continue to accept, at least publicly, the fundamental concepts of Western democracy, but have argued that present conditions are such that these principles cannot be implemented. This was the basic position of the Thai military after they overthrew the last elected government in 1971, of General Lon Nol after the ousting of Prince Sihanouk in 1970, and of President Marcos following the establishment of martial law in 1972. In each case the spokesmen of the new régime accused the fallen opposition of 'playing politics' with the security and development

36 'Pantja Sila Democracy' in operation: President Suharto addressing a session of the People's Congress of Indonesia.

of the country and each paid obeisance to the principles of democracy. At the same time, a different institutional pattern accompanied each *coup*. The Thai military eliminated the newly established Parliament and prepared to re-establish the old system of an appointed legislature; Lon Nol kept the National Assembly which was to prepare a new constitution; and Marcos set about changing the institutions of government within a supposed democratic framework. In a fashion each leader had disrupted old in-stitutions of varied democratic content and established a caretaker or

81

transitional government. While continuing to pay lip-service to democratic norms, these Thai, Cambodian and Filipino rulers were suspected of projecting a democratic ideology while preparing for an authoritarian system.

Three countries whose leaders had originally agreed with the precepts of Western democracy still follow its principles and, in varying degrees, its practices. Singapore, Malaysia and South Vietnam all declare their ideologies to be based upon liberal democratic precepts, while at the same time restricting political freedom in practice. Of these only Singapore has continuously maintained a relatively undiluted form of Western democracy. Malaysia suspended Parliament and certain political rights after the 1969 communal riots and in South Vietnam the generals eliminated the few concessions to democratic appearances granted under the Diem régime after his death in 1963. In each case democratic ideology does not include complete freedom for the opposition as this is defined in Western Europe. In Singapore politicians have been jailed, in Malaysia criticism of other races or fundamental government policy is prohibited and in South Vietnam newspapers have been closed and politicians arrested, particularly for making statements with regard to the war. All three countries refuse to allow Communists to participate openly in politics. At the same time, in none of them would the leadership publicly reject democracy as an unsuitable system of government.

In sum then, even the lip-service paid to democratic values has sharply diminished in the generation since 1945. Even where democracy continues to be practised the Western legacy has given way to indigenous roots. Rarely now are European or American writers quoted as democratic authorities, as national leaders have become the fountainheads of ideology.

Socialism remains an important element in the national ideologies of only four states, and even in these four it has taken on considerable local coloration or been severely diluted. It plays only a minor role or none at all in the national ideologies of Thailand, Laos, Malaysia, the Philippines, Cambodia and South Vietnam. In all of these six countries, however, insurgent groups proclaim one form or another of Marxism-Leninism. The Communist Party is engaged in guerrilla activities in Malaysia, Communist-led and supported local forces are to be found in Laos, Thailand, Cambodia, South Vietnam and the Philippines and in 1972 foreign Communist troops were fighting the right-wing governments of Laos, Cambodia and South Vietnam. It should be emphasized that not all insurgents were Communists or other types of Marxist, but in each case the articulate opposition professed Marxist principles. The fact that all called themselves 'Socialist' may have been a factor in influencing public opinion in their favour.

Of the other four countries, none still holds to an undiluted form of the Socialist principles they declared at the time of independence. North Vietnam stands fast as a Socialist state founded upon the tenets of Marxism-Leninism, but with some re-evaluation based upon the thoughts of Ho Chi Minh and other Vietnamese theorists. Party workers have been warned not to follow slavishly the words and themes of foreign comrades and there have been attacks upon those who have accused the party of lacking creativity and inventiveness. A definition of the exact nature of the domestic government must probably await more stable conditions of peace in Indo-China, but meanwhile its leaders still proclaim their adherence to Marxism-Leninism, defined in indigenous terms and conditions.

37 Ho Chi Minh portrayed as the inspiration of his country's troops. Ho's leadership of North Vietnam survived relatively uncontested from 1945 until his death in 1969.

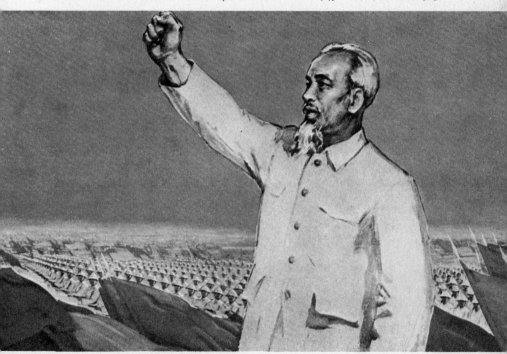

38–39 The Vietnam War through Communist eyes: left, children in the North huddle in a ditch during an American bombing raid; right, Cuban poster depicting the brutal American aggressor, directed by capitalist interests. For the world Vietnam has become synonymous with the tragic and wasteful suffering engendered when the cold war becomes 'hot'.

The most striking change in the Socialist ideology expressed in the 1940s took place in Burma after the 1962 military *coup* which rejected the evolutionary democratic Socialism of U Nu in favour of the revolutionary 'Burmese Way to Socialism'. The new ideology is based upon an intertwining of Marxist and indigenous roots, described as 'the planned proportional development of all the national productive forces'.[11] Although critics have described the realization of these principles as 'unplanned disproportional development', the Revolutionary Council of Burma demanded the nationalization of all vital means of production and distribution, introduced the principle of work according to ability and pay according to quality and quantity, and recognized the workers and peasants as the vanguard and custodians of the new Socialist state. In practice this has meant nationalization of foreign interests, wholesale and retail stores and co-operatives, control over distribution and marketing systems and the establishment of 'People's Stores' to distribute goods. While the military reduced some of the excesses of nationalization in the ensuing decade, the fundamental thrust of the nation's ideology remains one of radical socialization based upon the assumption that, since man is naturally self-seeking, self-interest and social interest must be correlated by the governments and that 'only when exploitation of many by one man is brought to an end and Socialist economy based on justice is established . . . only then can an affluent stage of development be reached.'[12]

Singapore remains a mixture of Socialist welfare ideology and a capitalist economy. Changes in ideology have, perhaps, been more from the early assessment of what an independent Singapore under Prime Minister Lee Kuan Yew would be like to the reality that followed. Lee's statements prior to independence appeared to anticipate a major movement towards a Socialist economy and the end of island's commercial importance. Instead, there has been the acceptance and encouragement of foreign and local capital alongside some of the most far-reaching welfare programmes in South-East Asia.

Finally, independent Indonesia has experienced a series of changes in the meaning of Socialism. After Sukarno's original support for social justice, the country entered a period when Socialism was muted as an article of faith. However, with the advent of Guided Democracy Socialism again took a central place. This time it was anti-imperialist and anti-capitalist, spiritual rather than material, and claimed to express the need for a 'Socialist society'. Yet the spokesmen for the new ideology refused to describe it as a 'definite system, the full details of which are already known'.

40 Burma's 'Way to Socialism' involved nationalization of all vital means of production and distribution, including – as seen here – breweries and distilleries.

Instead Sukarno spoke in romantic terms, calling on the people to 'march on towards the Dawn of Socialism which has already arisen on the Indonesian horizon' and the need for 'Indonesian identity', 'human values', 'economic democracy', and the eradication of 'exploitation de l'homme par l'homme', etc.

With the demise of Sukarno, Indonesian Socialism entered another phase. In practice, the new Suharto government turned from rejection of foreign capital and emphasis upon ideological slogans to an encouragement of Western investors and attention to the pragmatic problems involved in development. Socialism as a concept lost its central role, although social justice remained an announced public goal. Sukarno's emotional anti-capitalism and anti-imperialism were played down in the nation's effort to develop with the support of Western investors and aid.

If Western democracy had lost many of its early adherents and Socialism was largely restricted to insurgent groups, minority parties and only a few national ideologies, what of the third part of the trinity, nationalism? We discussed the nationalism of the 1940s in terms of anti-colonialism, unity and non-aggression. Anti-colonialism is no longer the central theme of nationalism that it once was, although neo-colonialism continues to be viewed as a possible danger. It is true that some countries have gone through periods of virulent anti-colonialism in the intervening years since the war, but the generation since independence has tended to have diluted memories of the colonial era and demands for economic development have forced the ruling élites into more pragmatic approaches towards international investors. However, the anti-colonial aspect of nationalism in particular shows the heterogeneous character of the post-war experiences of the South-East Asian states, as an examination of some of its more salient features shows.

Burma under Ne Win and Indonesia in the days of Sukarno display the strongest anti-Westernism, each country in its own distinct fashion. After 1962 Burma withdrew into its shell, rejecting what it considered to be decadent Western practices such as beauty contests and horse-racing. More important, the country became a recluse, refusing to allow in tourists for more than twenty-four hours and closing itself off to 'insidious' intellectual and cultural influences. In the process such organs as the United States Information Library, the British Council and foundations for international interchange were eliminated. Although there has been some loosening of regulations, Burma remains a hermit among South-East Asian nations. Indonesia under Sukarno was defiantly anti-Western, damning both economic and cultural 'neo-colonialism'. Sukarno nationalized Dutch and British firms, told the Americans to 'Go to hell with your foreign aid', and warned his people 'Why is it that amongst you many do not oppose cultural imperialism? Why is it that amongst you many still like to indulge in rock 'n roll, to "dance" à la cha-cha-cha, to make crazy mixed-up noises called music, and more of the same?'[13]

Most South-East Asian states, however, retreated from strong anti-colonialism, restricting their attacks to specific aspects of Western political and cultural intervention. Countries which have housed American military bases such as Vietnam, Thailand and the Philippines have objected to the activities of unthinking foreign soldiers and the proliferation of bars, prostitutes, night-clubs, etc. to cater to their desires.

One Thai newspaper editor attacked Americans for 'their shameless custom of kissing and hugging in public places, and other behavior no better than that of savage beasts', and for 'influencing Thai youths into

88

41 A young Malaysian family out shopping in a contemporary Kuala Lumpur supermarket. The capitalist economies and relative stability of Malaysia and Singapore have brought a steady rise in living standards and concomitant Westernization.

42 In the Philippines Western influence, represented here by a Coca-Cola sign in the small village of Lamitan on Basilan Island, is all-pervasive.

following and indulging in deteriorated conduct.'[14] The presence of military bases has irritated relations with the surrounding population and has been a sore point especially between the United States and the Philippines. Motion pictures, Western television programmes, advertisements for modern goods have all been seen as a danger to national cultural values.

Finally, the influx of foreign capital has been viewed by many as the most dangerous form of neo-colonialism and the élites of the region have tried hard to make some sort of compromise between the need for foreign investment and the desire to protect the national interest. In Burma, North Vietnam and Sukarno's Indonesia this meant an effort to replace the foreigner, while in other states the demand for outside aid has led to an uneasy acceptance of Western capital. In the latter cases, there have been restrictions on the percentage of foreign capital allowed in, laws to compel foreign corporations to train nationals at all levels, and prohibitions on international investment in areas of particular national interest. Today, apart from Burma and North Vietnam, all states recognize the need to deal with the former colonial powers, and particularly Japan, although there remains an almost universal fear of neo-colonialism, both economic and cultural.

The drive towards national unity engrossed the leadership of most of South-East Asia in the generation following independence and is still the vital element in the nationalist ideology of most countries in the region. The clearest sign of this is a heightened sense of national awareness. The passing years have seen a growing awareness of nationhood among the peoples of the various countries. The development of new road and air networks, wide distribution of radios (and particularly transistors in areas without electricity) and increased literacy resulting in a larger reading public have all helped to break down local parochialism. For the first time in history there have been elections for national office throughout South-East Asia, and these have forced the voter to consider country-wide issues and made politicians widen their political horizons. Even wars such as those in Indo-China have increased urbanization, technology and nationalist propaganda, all heightening national awareness.

At the same time, state boundaries have now largely been settled and the only outright vestige of colonialism in the region is tiny Portuguese Timor. Only in Indo-China do the borders between states remain unsettled. The two major inter-state conflicts over territory have largely been resolved. West Irian, which was held by the Dutch after the rest of the East Indies had won independence and had exacerbated Dutch-Indonesian relations for more than a decade, came under Indonesian suzerainty in 1962. North Borneo was the object of international tension between Malaysia and the Philippines when the former incorporated the British colony in 1963, but although relations between the two states were broken off for a period the issue is no longer a major point of contention. Thus, the basic frontiers of the region appear set – at least for the immediate future. However, the combination of increased awareness of nationhood and the establishment of firm international boundaries has not managed to eliminate severe internal conflicts.

Dissident groups still operate within individual countries and civil war between governments and ethnic and regional minorities is a reality in almost every state in the region. In Burma, Shans, Kachins, Karens and Communists are still at war with Rangoon. In Thailand the 1960s saw regional insurgency and unrest among the minority peoples in the north, north-east and south, and Indo-China was still the scene of ideological, tribal and regional conflict at the beginning of the 1970s. In the Philippines there was ideological unrest in the northern islands and trouble with Moro dissidents on Mindanao. Malaysia faced a small Malayan Communist Party guerrilla group on the peninsula and insurgents in east Malaysia. Only Indonesia, after the virtual extermination of the Communist Party, appeared relatively quiet, and even here there were isolated Communist disturbances. In these circumstances it is little wonder that unity is given continued emphasis as the central theme of nationalist ideology throughout South-East Asia.

In 1972 the principle of non-aggression which had been a characteristic feature of early nationalism was still maintained, although there were periods in the intervening years when the situation was different. Critics of President Sukarno charged him with attempting to expand his country's influence and territory through the so-called 'confrontation' with Malaysia. Sukarno fought on the side of dissidents in northern Borneo, arguing that he was protecting the people's right of self-determination against Malaysian neo-colonialism. It is difficult to ascertain Sukarno's real designs, although neighbours were disturbed when he told his people that 'We are no second-rate nation, our Nation is Great, with Great Ambitions, Great Ideals, Great Creative Power, and Great Tenacity.'[15] Even more obscure are the hidden motives for the internecine conflicts in Indo-China where government and opposition forces in Laos, Cambodia and Vietnam accuse one another of expansionism and of plotting with foreign powers for the destruction of their enemies.

43 The new national awareness: girls parade in a celebration of the first anniversary of Cambodian independence.

At the present time, however, the national leadership in most of the lands of South-East Asia regards aggression against another independent state as no part of its nationalist ideology. The more virulent and aggressive period of post-war nationalism appears to have subsided. As the newly emancipated states of South-East Asia mature and the memories of colonialism and earlier revolutionary heroes decline, their governing élites are becoming less backward-looking and more involved in coping with pressing contemporary issues and problems. At present their most important concern is probably the institutionalization of nationhood and the uniting of conflicting groups. Thus, although the fear of neo-colonialism remains a potent factor throughout the region, it would seem that nationalism is now developing into a much more positive force.

What, then, has become of the role of ideology in general in the politics of South-East Asia? It would seem that, on the whole, we can trace a line of evolution which holds for most of the region. First, there was the initial euphoria of independence and nationalism. Then almost all countries went through a phase, lasting between five and ten years, when decision-making was concentrated on specific practical problems, and ideology tended to be down-graded. Caught up in the challenge of economic development and nation-building the ruling classes had not much time for slogans. As one spokesman of the ruling Alliance Party of Malaya explained, 'Dogmatism is not good, often dogmatism sacrifices pragmatism.'[16]

During the succeeding decade ideology took on a new force. In Burma the military began developing its own ideological concepts culminating in the Burmese Way to Socialism. The South Vietnamese leader, Ngo Dinh Diem, expanded upon his doctrine of 'personalism' until his death in 1963. In North Vietnam, which for a period after 1954 had concentrated on rehabilitation at home, the renewed drive to reunite the divided country after 1960 again revived ideological fervour. In Indonesia Sukarno placed increasing stress on ideology, declaring in 1960 that 'the torrent of history shows clearly that all nations need some conception and ideal'. 'When we had entered the period of implementation of the Message of Suffering of the people,' he subsequently declared, 'the National Concept was absolutely essential.' Late in the 1960s even Malaysia launched upon a national ideology called Rukunegara ('the fundamental doctrine of the state') which emphasized loyalty to the constitution, unity and dedication to the rule of law.

The reasons for this increased emphasis on ideology can be found in the basic difficulties in which the governing élites found themselves involved. Bedevilled by problems of economic development and national unity, they not unexpectedly sought an emotional cement to consolidate the will of their people. As the Ministry of National Unity of Malaysia explained, the 'principles and norms against which plans and actions can be evaluated and the dynamic to motivate movements can only be effectively provided if there is a NATIONAL IDEOLOGY clearly declared and overarching, transcending the affiliations of race, religion, cultural, class and political parties.'[17]

For most of South-East Asia, however, ideology did not prove to be an effective means of binding a nation together and in recent years there has been decidedly less emphasis upon it. It is certainly not dead, however, and the ruling élites of North Vietnam, Malaysia and Burma still regard it as important; but pragmatic economics and politics appear to be the dominant strains in the region at the present juncture. In part this may also be due to the disappearance from the scene, by death or otherwise, of the great ideologues, such as U Nu, Ngo Dinh Diem, Sukarno and Ho Chi Minh. The leaders who have followed have been more in the mould of the bureaucrats who succeeded Stalin in the Soviet Union.

In sum, the legacy of democracy, Socialism and nationalism left over from the colonial and nationalist periods has been transformed by the post-war experiences and indigenous environmental forces of individual countries. No longer are the tenets of European writers and early nationalist ideologues accepted without question. South-East Asia has sufficiently matured to design its own concepts interweaving foreign ideas with indigenous traditions.

44 King Bhumibol Adulyadej of Thailand; traditional pomp of an order now unique in South-East Asia is a valuable tool in strengthening national pride.

5 The Institutional Legacy

If there have been changes in ideology, the same is true of the institutional legacy of the colonial and early nationalist periods. We shall attempt in what follows to see how far the original institutions still remain in existence and how far they continue to perform the functions for which they were originally intended. Four particular questions will be studied: the relations of executive and legislature, the judiciary, civil relations between the civil government and the military, and the constitution.

THE RISE OF EXECUTIVE POWER

The new states of South-East Asia were successors to European and American colonial administrations and were led by men heavily influenced by the intellectual currents present in the West. Volksraads, legislative councils and other legislative bodies were developing during the last years of the colonial era. The Philippines, Burma and Malaya had their own indigenous executives even prior to independence. When we combine this experience with the initial attraction of democratic ideology, it is not surprising that the legislative-executive institutions formed at independence were largely copies of Western models.

For the former colonies of the United Kingdom, France and the Netherlands, the inherited institutional arrangement was parliamentary, with some consideration given to local conditions. Parliament was elected by the people, the prime minister and cabinet were responsible to it, and the titular head, president or monarch, had ceremonial as well as restricted constitutional tasks. Naturally there were local variations. The number, size, powers and methods of the Houses differed. For example, Burma's second chamber had members assigned to it by the different communities in the land, while Indonesia had but one House. Similarly, the electoral systems usually followed those of the mother country; the former British colonies tended to use single-member districts while Indonesia employed proportional representation.

The major differences between governments in the region revolved round the role and powers of the titular head of state. In Laos, Cambodia, Thailand and Malaysia the system was monarchical and the monarchs

97

officially held powers similar to those of their European counterparts, with variations dependent upon the personal magnetism of the individual ruler. A somewhat unusual system was constituted in Malaya where the state sultans chose from among their own number one who was to become king for a term of five years. Apart from the Philippines, the remaining states of South-East Asia elected presidents who were to perform functions mirroring those of the presidents of European republics, that is, their power was primarily ceremonial. In the Burmese case the president was also symbolic of national unity and thus alternately chosen from different communal groups. The one case where the titular head also held very real powers was in Indonesia. Here the 1950 constitution and even more the original 1945 constitution both vested the president with more than nominal powers, and under Sukarno even these were greatly expanded until in the end he had secured real control of appointments and veto powers.

The institutions of the Philippines, modelled on those of the United States, were unique in the area. Here a congressional-presidential system was instituted, closely moulded after the American one. Two houses of congress were elected, one by district and the other at large. A nationally elected president was given greater prerogatives than in the American system, and a unitary structure rather than a federal one centralized power more than in the United States. There were other variations, but the American influence was unmistakable.

On the surface, therefore, it is remarkable how closely the nationalists modelled their initial institutions after the countries from which they had so vigorously sought freedom. But if we look more closely there are many grounds for thinking that the legislative and executive institutions set up at the time of independence were mere shells which did not reflect real power relationships, and this conclusion is borne out by the speed with which they were later transformed. In fact the succeeding years saw two general trends, an increase in the power of the executive and the weakening of legislative prerogatives. In every country in the area the executive grew stronger in the years following independence. Prime ministers and presidents by-passed or reinterpreted constitutional limitations to reinforce their positions. In Burma, U Nu rarely deigned to appear before Parliament, in Indo-China national assemblies became mere appendages of strong national leaders such as Sihanouk and Diem, while in Indonesia Sukarno gradually built up his position through the 1950s until he was prepared to challenge the very existence of the Indonesian Parliament. In turn, the legislatures became less and less the real centres of power, turning

45 Symbols of the main political parties displayed before the first Indonesian general election in 1955. Western-style party politics did not, however, survive the early years of Sukarno's régime.

instead into bodies for rubber-stamping decisions made elsewhere or wasting themselves in seemingly fruitless conflicts with strong executives.

The reasons for these developments are to be found in weak party structures, the strong personalities of leaders, the dominance of a single party and the inexperience of the members of the legislature. In Burma, Singapore, Malaysia, the Philippines and the Indo-Chinese states the heads of government usually maintained overwhelming majorities in their legislatures. This often allowed them to ignore parliament or congress and go their own way. However, in most countries in the region even this centralization of power did not prove adequate for the purposes of those seeking to establish a strong national leadership, and by the 1970s most of the original institutions had been either abandoned or their functions severely altered.

In Burma, Thailand and the Philippines the institutions set up at the time of independence have been permanently or temporarily abandoned. With the 1962 *coup* in Burma, Parliament was disbanded, the prime minister and cabinet jailed and a military-dominated Revolutionary Council established to exercise all executive and legislative powers. A decade later the Revolutionary Council still performed these functions. The 1971 *coup* in Thailand saw a similar suspension of Parliament; here the new military junta called itself the National Executive Council and ruled by decree. The constitution has been abrogated and it is too early to know what structures, if any, will be formed to take its place. The 1972 *coup* in the Philippines has also left a question-mark overhanging the nature of the structure of government, although it is certain that the previous executive and legislative institutions will be basically transformed. In all these three countries, in short, the Western legacy has been rejected.

The non-Communist Indo-Chinese states and Indonesia, on the other hand, still have institutions which superficially resemble those at the time of independence. To be sure, there have been periods when civilian government has been suspended by the military and in most cases there has been some restructuring of the basic institutions. The older parliamentary pattern is still to be found, but the functions of the legislature and executive are very different from those ideally supposed to exist in Western democracies. Parliament rarely challenges the national leader, whose power has been buttressed by new constitutional and political forces. Instead, it performs secondary functions, such as giving an appearance of legitimacy to the government in the eyes of domestic and more particularly of foreign observers, allowing political groups inside the country a safety-valve, and maintaining some sort of communication between the ruling élite and the rest of society. Parliament in the Indo-Chinese states has not been completely powerless, as is evidenced by effective votes of no confidence in government ministers passed in Cambodia and by the defeat of important Bills in the Vietnamese National Assembly. However, the constitutional powers of strong men like Lon Nol and Thieu, combined with the backing they receive from the military and foreign governments, provide effective means of overwhelming recalcitrant legislatures.

Indonesia has experienced more than one restructuring of its political institutions since independence. Starting out with a generally orthodox parliamentary system with a strong president, it passed through 'Guided Democracy' with all essential power in the hands of Sukarno and a weak, primarily consultative, appointed legislature, to the present so-called 'Pantja Sila Democracy'. As now operating, this includes a Parliament of 460 members, 100 of whom are appointed by President Suharto (75 of the 100 are drawn from the military). The executive is the most powerful

— Как видите, сэр, южные вьетнамцы обеими руками за режим Тхиеу — Ки.

46 Cartoon from the Russian magazine *Krokodil* on the South Vietnamese elections of 1967: 'You see, sir,' says General Westmoreland to an American capitalist, 'The South Vietnamese are voting in favour of Thieu's régime with both hands!'

47 The bewigged President of the Malaysian Senate chats with the Speaker of the Lower House. The more bizarre aspects of their European legacy nevertheless often reflect a genuine desire to adopt Western legislative and constitutional practices.

element in the system, both constitutionally and politically, and all would agree that the institutional arrangements when combined with the overwhelming majority secured by the government in the last parliamentary elections (327 including appointed members) make the legislative arm of the government very weak indeed.

What we appear to have in these countries are semi-authoritarian régimes maintaining some semblance of parliamentary government. In no case would one expect the legislatures effectively to challenge the power of the military-backed leaders. Were they to do so, it is not unlikely that they would follow the post-war pattern of Thailand, where the armed forces have regularly stepped in to dissolve political institutions when Parliament has chosen to flex its muscles.

Malaysia and Singapore are the only two countries in the region where the executive and legislative institutions remain largely unchanged and continue on the whole to perform the functions originally intended. Neither has experienced a change in government at the national level to test the system, although the opposition has controlled some of the constituent states of the Malaysian Federation in the past. It should also be noted that the government of Malaysia saw fit to suspend Parliament for two years and rule by decree. However, parliamentary institutions as currently operating have not changed drastically in the years since independence. The major danger continues to be the difficulty of operating a meaningful parliamentary system when the electoral mandate of the majority party is so great as to deny effective opposition. This problem has been particularly acute in Singapore where there has been only token parliamentary opposition and at times none at all. Compared with their neighbours, however, Malaysia and Singapore have displayed remarkable continuity.

THE DETERIORATION OF JUDICIAL INDEPENDENCE

Superficially it has sometimes appeared that the judiciary of South-East Asia was copying too much from the West. The sight of judges in a tropical country wearing wigs and robes seemed slightly ridiculous and somewhat impractical. Looking beyond these symbolic throwbacks, however, the first question to be asked is what is the legacy under consideration? The dual system of courts and law that functioned in so much of South-East Asia before 1941 and gave unequal treatment to litigants and prisoners according to their race and colour? Local traditional or religious law to which some attention was still paid in Moslem colonies? Or is the model one of the European judicial systems under which so many of the Asian political leaders received their early training?

Broadly speaking, the new governing élites attempted to follow Western judicial models, and naturally enough they tended to be based in each country upon the system in use in the former colonial power. This was to be expected, given the personal experience of those who set up the courts at the time of independence. In accordance with Western practice judicial institutions were to be independent of political influence and generally were constituted to protect that independence. This was particularly true of the high courts of Malaysia, Singapore, Burma and the Philippines. The judiciary did not fare so well in the former French colonies, however, where the heritage had not been one of judicial independence and the Departments of Justice were prepared to put pressure on judges under their control. In line with European models, the institutions established in South-East Asia also threw out the dual racial legal systems of the colonial period, although religious courts were allowed to function in several states.

In the first years after independence the system operated comparatively well. The higher courts in most cases displayed remarkable independence and there were major efforts to expand statutory and constitutional law. There were difficulties at lower levels, where corruption and political pressure were often present and Departments or Ministries of Justice were prone to transfer or promote individual judges for reasons other than merit or competence. On the whole, however, until other democratic institutions foundered, the courts continued to develop and gain experience.

The greatest danger to the independence and effectiveness of the judiciary came from the increasing power of strong political leaders and the entrance of the military into civil affairs. Even prior to the military *coups* which wracked the area, powerful politicians were beginning to influence courts to make decisions in their favour, by-passing the regular legal system and promulgating law through decree. In Indo-China and Indonesia in particular the position of the courts deteriorated sharply at this period, as opposition newspapers, political rivals and insurgents were subjected to an increasingly brutal régime of extra-legal violence. In time, the judicial systems of most of the states in the region came under direct attack. The establishment of martial law in Indonesia, Thailand, the Philippines and the Indo-Chinese countries led to the curtailment of civil rights which were never fully regained. With the 1962 *coup* in Burma the entire network of courts was reshaped and the high court disbanded. The long Indo-China war undermined whatever independence the judiciary of the area had previously possessed.

The rule of law is not dead in South-East Asia. Many of the institutions still function, if not with their former powers. An independent judiciary is largely a reality in Malaysia and Singapore. It would, however, be naïve to expect that the forces that brought about the demise of other democratic institutions would spare the judiciary, and in most countries where the military has gained control the changes have been very considerable.

THE RISE OF THE MILITARY

Every state in South-East Asia began independence with a firm belief in civilian control over the military. The role of the armed forces in achieving victory over colonialism in Burma, Indo-China and Indonesia was recognized and applauded and it was expected that they would be imbued with the national ideology. After all, members of the early ruling élites such as Giap and Aung San had led armies and very close relations between civil and military nationalists had existed during the Japanese occupation and the later struggles against colonialism. After independence, on the other hand, it was expected that the armed forces would accept the traditional role of political neutrality as practised in most of Western Europe and the United States. Both in constitutional law and in political philosophy the military was to be subject to civilian control. The constitutions of the period stated this quite clearly. For example, the Burmese constitution declared that 'supreme command of the armed forces shall be vested in the president' and 'shall be regulated by law', although the president was not actually to command the army. The 1950 Indonesian constitution similarly declared that the president was 'vested with supreme authority over the armed forces', a position that Sukarno attempted to exploit and expand. Whatever the ideological presuppositions otherwise passed on by the French, American, Dutch and British colonial régimes, a key principle in every case was the dominance of the civil authority. Even in North Vietnam, where the nationalist leadership rejected much of French political ideology, Communist doctrine laid down that the army was to be under the party.

In practice, the theory of the predominance of the civil authority over the military remains intact today only in Malaysia and Singapore. Neither of these countries appears to be in danger of falling under military rule and in both the supremacy of the civil authority is strictly enforced. Other states have experienced different histories. As early as the first decade after the war the role of the military was becoming a major issue of policy in Indonesia, parts of Indo-China, Burma and Thailand, and in succeeding years the relationship set up at independence collapsed. The turning-point was 1958. Starting in that year the armed forces in country after country began to assert their power in the civil field. It was in 1958 that General Ne Win and his fellow officers took over the Burmese prime ministership and other key offices, and though they restored civil government in 1960 it was only to return permanently in 1962. The ruling Revolutionary Council is almost entirely composed of army officers. In South Vietnam the assassination of Ngo Dinh Diem in 1963 inaugurated a decade of military dominance over South Vietnamese politics and from that time forward most major national and provincial offices have been controlled by members of the armed forces. In Indonesia, following the fall of Sukarno, General Suharto and his military colleagues claimed for themselves the large majority of key positions formerly held by civilians.

It is true that in many ways army control at the provincial level only formalized what had been a normal practice for more than a decade. Thailand has experienced almost continuous military rule since the Second World War and in fact a military man has occupied the position of prime minister for thirty-seven years since the revolution of 1932. After the overthrow of Sihanouk in 1970 the army increased its power in Cambodia and General Lon Nol emerged as the unquestioned leader. In Laos the army has long been a factor in national and provincial politics, with individual officers participating in the complex intrigues that appear to be an integral part of Laotian political life. In the early 1970s the civilian government again attempted to bring the armed services into subordination to it, although the internal tensions and necessities of war made this difficult. There are reports also that the long Indo-China war increased the political influence of the military elements in North Vietnam. Finally, the declaration of martial law by the Philippine President Marcos in 1972 gave a new role to a military that had previously remained politically neutral. Many observers noted the public efforts of Marcos to gain the allegiance and co-operation of key military officers.

In sum, civil control of the military has reached a low point in post-independent South-East Asia. Nor apparently is the situation affected by

48–50 The rise of the military: Opposite left, President Suharto receives an appropriate gift from a French visitor in an ironic reversal of the colonial Powers' earlier attempts to limit their subjects' access to armaments; right, General Ne Win, who set up a military caretaker government in Burma in 1958. Above, Prince Norodom Sihanouk of Cambodia, playboy turned friend of Mao, addresses a rally after his arrival in Peking following a military *coup* in his country.

the heritage left by the colonial powers, for ex-Dutch, ex-American, ex-French and ex-British territories have all undergone the same evolution. A not too subtle piece of advice heard in different variations throughout the region is that if you have a son who wants to be a president, cabinet minister, engineer, town-planner, health administrator, judge or entrepreneur, the important thing is to send him to a military academy first. It is the only way to reach the top. However, it must be recognized that the attainment of power by the military is only part of a general decay of constitutional government.

THE DECLINE OF CONSTITUTIONAL GOVERNMENT

Apart from setting out and defining the organization and functions of government, post-war constitutions have commonly been allotted two other roles. The first is to place limits on the powers of government, the second to set general goals towards which the people should aspire. The early constitutions of South-East Asia sought to achieve both goals. In each country the constitution set out the rights and duties of citizens and prescribed how the state was to operate. It can be argued that more often than not the rights and duties were aspirations rather than realities, but there was considerable early optimism about government limited by law and this lasted as late as 1960. Although, as has been pointed out above, strong leaders were expanding their power in the 1950s, the basic institutional arrangements generally remained intact and even when abandoned the hope was that their abrogation was but a temporary aberration.

The years since 1960 have proved that the early optimism was unjustified. Constitutional government no longer operates in Burma and Thailand even as a façade, while new arrangements have been promulgated or are in the process of preparation in South Vietnam, Indonesia, Cambodia and the Philippines. It is questionable, to say the least, whether the constitution actually limits the power of government in Laos and North Vietnam, and the situation under the new régimes in South Vietnam, Indonesia and Cambodia appears to be basically similar. What is certain is that none of these countries have constitutions which command the whole-hearted support and respect of the leadership or population and in all probability their disappearance would not be deeply mourned. This leaves us once again with Malaysia and Singapore as the exceptions, and of these the former suspended its constitution at a time of crisis. No doubt it would be foolish to expect the constitutions of South-East Asia to be treated with the same reverence as is the constitution of the United States, but it is significant that we do not find among South-East Asians even the attitude prevalent in Latin America, where military *coups* are justified as a defence of constitutional government and constitutional change is explained in terms relevant to the basic laws of the land.

As the preceding analysis shows, except in Malaysia and Singapore the institutional legacies of the colonial and early nationalist periods have proved extremely weak. Whether we take as our point of reference the relations of legislature and executive, judicial or military institutions, or constitutional law, no fewer than eight countries in South-East Asia have either abandoned their original post-independence structures or changed their functions while retaining the façade of the old system. Rather than analysing the particular reasons for the failure of the early post-independence institutions to take root in the majority of the countries of the area it is more pertinent to ask why Singapore and Malaysia have succeeded in maintaining the original patterns largely intact.

Six reasons can be put forward to explain the exceptional position of Malaysia and Singapore, though taken separately none probably affords a complete answer. In fact, what has differentiated their history from that of the other countries of the region is probably a combination of several different factors. These include a longer period of colonial rule after the war, the high quality of the civil service, a pragmatic approach to political problems, a stable party structure, higher economic standards than in most other parts of South-East Asia and the absence of major internal and external challenges.

Malaysia and Singapore were the last countries in the region to receive independence. During the decade of colonial rule after the war the British deliberately prepared their colonies to take over self-government and were able to rehabilitate them after the destruction caused by the war and the Japanese occupation. They also aided in putting down local insurgents prior to independence, thereby ridding their colonies of a problem faced by most of the other states in their first unstable years of freedom.

The Malayan peninsula and Singapore were also blessed with one of the best civil services in the area. The indigenous political leaders were relatively willing to co-operate with the colonial administration, and this made it possible to employ European expatriates in certain positions until a new cadre of native administrators had been built up, a possibility not always present elsewhere. This provided the new administrative élite with an efficient bureaucratic infrastructure capable of carrying out its programmes. The significance of this factor becomes obvious when we recall the heavy

51 Pragmatic capitalism: Tengku Abdul Rahman opens a new oil refinery at Port Dickson, Malaysia.

losses of trained personnel in Burma through war, nationalist resistance and revolt, or the almost total lack of preparation, to say nothing of the frequent arrest of educated nationalists and the policy of non-cooperation, that characterized French and Dutch colonial government. There is no doubt that Singapore and Malaysia were even better off in this respect than independent Thailand. The author has travelled widely in both areas and has repeatedly observed the higher quality and greater quantity of civil servants in rural Malaysia by comparison with rural Thailand. The very fact that Thai bureaucrats have been sent to Malaysia to study the techniques and administration of economic development is itself a good indication of the superiority of the latter.

The pragmatic, non-ideological approach of Tengku Abdul Rahman, Tun Razak and Lee Kuan Yew was also a significant factor. Certainly it contrasted markedly with the attitude of ideologues such as U Nu,

52 Idealistic nationalism: U Nu of Burma caricatured giving funds for the Sixth
Buddhist Synod while businessmen appeal in vain for similar aid.

Sukarno, Ne Win, Ngo Dinh Diem and Ho Chi Minh. None of the former
would declare, as did Sukarno, that economic development has nothing to
do with a nation's greatness. One has only to compare U Nu's drive to build
tens of thousands of sand pagodas as an act of religious merit with the unwillingness of the Malaysian government to close all government offices on
the Moslem day of prayer because it would injure the country's external
trade to see the difference. Equally significant, when compared with the
rooted hostility of most South-East Asian leaders to the presence of foreign
bases, were Lee Kuan Yew's efforts to induce the British to retain a major
naval base at Singapore for economic reasons. It is possible to question the
lack of commitment of some of these pragmatic leaders, and their com-
promises with neo-colonialism and imperialism, but there is no doubt that
they contributed to more effective economic development and in this
way helped to forestall political dissatisfaction.

III

The dominance of a single party in both states was a further factor contributing to political stability, at least in so far as it diminished the fears of the ruling élites and provided continuity in policy. The very fact that there was no effective challenge to Lee Kuan Yew's People Action Party weakened demands for the outlawing of the opposition. For years the ruling Alliance Party of Malaysia felt secure behind heavy parliamentary majorities. The severe losses suffered by the party in the 1969 general elections and the riots that ensued led to the suspension of democratic institutions. Currently efforts are being made to form coalition governments with the opposition parties in the different states of the Federation, the object, no doubt, being to stabilize the system if possible by reducing the domestic challenges to the Alliance leaders. Whether this expedient will produce a long-term solution is, of course, another question.

Nevertheless, even allowing for the setback in Malaysia after 1969, the experience of that country and of Singapore compares markedly with the chronic party instability elsewhere. The 1958 *coup* in Burma arose out of a split in the ruling AFPFL. The more than two dozen parties that gained parliamentary representation in the 1955 Indonesian elections immobilized the political system, giving Sukarno ample justification for inaugurating 'Guided Democracy'. In Thailand the increase in the parliamentary vote against the party run by the military establishment was the direct cause of the 1971 *coup d'état*. A trained, pragmatic leadership is no guarantee against military intervention, but it helps to maintain the party system, particularly if it is combined with a successful economic policy.

Here the record of Malaysia and Singapore is good. Ever since their post-war rehabilitation they have continued to have the highest *per capita* Gross National Product of all the countries in South-East Asia. With a combined population of less than fourteen million the two countries have attained a combined GNP larger than that of any country except the Philippines, with more than twice their population, and Indonesia with a population in excess of a hundred million. The *per capita* comparison is even more striking. On this basis Malaysia and Singapore tower above all their neighbours. While income per head in the relatively rich Philippines hovers around $200, and elsewhere the average is under $150 per annum, in Singapore it is over $100 and in Malaysia over $400 per annum. Moreover, although there are great disparities in income in both countries, major efforts have been made to correct the situation. In Malaysia this has taken the form of programmes to aid the poorer, agricultural Malays, while in Singapore the government has developed large-scale housing and other welfare projects.

53 The Asia Insurance building on the waterfront towers over Singapore as an impressive symbol of the nation's commitment to progress and a capitalist economy.

Finally, Malaysia and Singapore have been fortunate in so far as neither has suffered from major internal disturbances or foreign wars. It is true that both countries have experienced communal riots but in neither did casualties amount to more than a thousand dead. The confrontation with Indonesia also involved Malaysia in international conflict but this largely guerrilla war was confined in the main to the outlying Borneo territories and never really touched West Malaysia. Present insurgent activity is limited to infrequent actions in Borneo and against the Malayan Communist Party residing in southern Thailand. It is only necessary to compare this relative peace with the generation of civil war and foreign intervention suffered by Burma, Laos and Vietnam, with the rebellions in Indonesia in the 1950s and the murder of hundreds of thousands of Communists and Communist supporters in 1965–66, or with the war that has engulfed Cambodia since 1970, to see how important a factor it is.

The author is not so sanguine as to believe that the existing institutions in Malaysia and Singapore are permanently set, although there are certainly more reasons to be optimistic about their future than about that of most of their neighbours. However, so long as major economic and social disparities exist between the different races living in Malaysia the conditions are present for a communal conflagration that could once again result in the suspension, if not the total abrogation, of democratic processes and institutions. The social legacy of the past has left South-East Asia with a series of unresolved tensions which in the long run may prove to be its most intractable and explosive problems.

6 The Social Legacy

In the period prior to independence education was a privilege for the children of the European ruling class and a small minority of Asians. The level of literacy in most countries varied between 10 and 40 per cent and only a small percentage of the privileged few received more than four years of schooling. Except in the Philippines, higher education was a phenomenon of the period after the First World War and only a few hundred graduated in any given year. Widening the gap was the fact that post-primary education was centred almost entirely in the cities. Health services were also primarily confined to urban areas, although the colonial administrations had greatly reduced infant mortality and death-rates in general. In fact, their success in this respect resulted in a population explosion throughout the region.

Colonialism and early nationalism did not eliminate and often exacerbated communal tensions. In earlier chapters we have noted the impact of policies of indirect rule, divisions between Christians and other religious groups, particularly Buddhists, hostility towards minority communities, particularly the Chinese, who were often treated as pariahs, and inter-regional conflicts. At the same time increasing disparities were emerging between the more industrialized and Westernized urban populations and the agricultural, more traditional and isolated rural peasants.

The entire region was in an era of transition during the inter-war years, and this process was accelerated by the Japanese occupation and the post-war nationalist struggles. South-East Asia is still undergoing massive change as modernization is proceeding, often in spite of growing suspicion of the validity of Western political and human values.

POST-INDEPENDENCE SOCIAL DEVELOPMENTS

If we compare the situation today with that of a generation ago, the first point to stress is the weight given to education by the new independent governments. Understandably, they saw in a literate and trained population the foundation for more active participation in politics and for more

54–57 All the newly independent governments in South-East Asia have recognized the importance of education, though the resultant measures have met with varying degrees of success. Left, a girls' secondary school in Saigon and (below) a dancing class in a Thai kindergarten. Right, the Vice-Chancellor of the University of Singapore speaks on Graduation Day; below, peasants attending a literacy class in Malaya.

rapid economic development. By 1960 only Cambodia admitted to a literacy rate of under 40 per cent, while Burma, the Philippines, Malaysia, Singapore and Thailand all claimed that a majority of their adult populations could read and write. These figures may be somewhat suspect, and actual illiteracy is probably higher. However, literacy is generally considered a sign of modernization and governments annually report increased percentages, to the point where in 1965 Sukarno announced that 100 per cent of Indonesians between thirteen and forty-five were literate. In any case there is no doubt whatever that major strides forward have been made. In 1940, for example, the Dutch East Indies had 2,000,000 children in primary schools and only 26,000 in secondary schools. Ten years after the war there were 7,400,000 in primary grades and 636,000 in secondary schools. Malaya had 870,000 students in all departments in 1947 and Malaysia over 2,000,000 in 1972.

The training of a sizable number of graduates from institutions of higher learning who could man the upper echelons of the civil service and provide the professional personnel necessary to implement the governments' programmes was of central importance for the development of the new states. We have previously noted the paucity of such training in the pre-war years, and such as there was largely came to a halt during the Japanese occupation. In the first years of independence, institutions of higher learning proliferated, sometimes without adequate teaching staffs or facilities. However, the need was great. For example, Cambodia had no more than eight hundred students in technical schools and a single Buddhist university as late as 1957–58, Laos opened its first institution of higher learning in 1954, and Malaya had to depend upon the university in Singapore until the 1950s. Now every country has its colleges, universities and technical schools, numbering from five in Laos to over a hundred in Indonesia and more than seven hundred in the Philippines. These vary from large, relatively high-quality institutions such as the University of Malaya or Chulalongkorn University in Bangkok to the diploma mills of the Philippines.

Even with this increase in educational opportunities, many basic problems remain. South-East Asia has a long way to go to reach the 98 per cent literacy rate of Japan. Of greater significance is the persistence of gross internal disparities. The pre-war structure which limited post-primary schooling to the very few has continued. For example, in 1961 it was reported that 83·6 per cent of Thai children were in the equivalent of the American first through fourth grades, only 1·5 per cent in the last two years of secondary school, and a mere 0·8 per cent in colleges or universities.

58 A co-educational biology class at Hué University, South Vietnam.

Moreover, this pattern accentuates the disparities between the rural areas and the urban, since the centres of educational opportunity at the secondary level are usually in urban areas. Without a solid secondary schooling the student is not qualified for university training, and without a diploma from one of the institutions of higher learning he is likely to be frozen out of the upper echelons of the bureaucracy and the professions. Meanwhile, the sons and daughters of the bureaucratic, professional and commercial élite can afford to attend the prestigious schools that funnel students into the best universities at home and abroad. While, therefore, education at all levels has burgeoned, quality schooling in South-East Asia is still a prerogative of the few.

A somewhat similar situation exists in the health service. After independence, medical facilities were expanded in every country. The colonial régimes had left few trained indigenous medical officers in most countries of the region. In Cambodia there were only eight non-military doctors in 1955. French Indo-China as a whole had a pre-war ratio of one doctor for 38,000 people, and as late as the mid-1950s there was still only one doctor for every 60,000 persons in Indonesia. These figures were improved upon

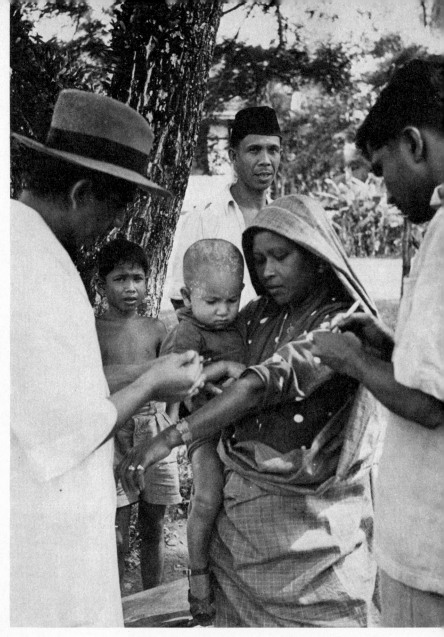

59 A Malaysian mother and her children being vaccinated in the open air. Through-out South-East Asia, rural areas tend to be starved of medical facilities, most doctors preferring to live and work in the cities.

in succeeding years, but in most countries the situation remained discouraging. The ratios of doctors to population ranged from one to 1,700 in the Philippines and one to 2,300 in Singapore to one to 31,000 in Cambodia, one to 37,000 in Laos and one to 41,000 in Indonesia. This situation was somewhat mitigated by the development of 'bare-foot doctors' and other minimally trained medical technicians as well as major programmes against dangerous diseases such as malaria and cholera. As a result, medical statistics show a drop in crude death-rates and a rise in life expectancy of from five to ten years, if one can believe the figures. However, life expectancy for males still ranges from a low of approximately 42 years in Cambodia to a high of 55·5 years in Malaysia, well below the level of 67·7 in Japan. What these figures would be like if adequate cognizance of deaths in war were included we do not know.

Here again, there are major disparities between rural and urban areas. Doctors, nurses and medical facilities tend to be concentrated in the large cities, so that over-all statistics on doctor-to-population ratios are extremely deceptive. For example, during the 1960s approximately two-thirds of the doctors and nurses of Thailand practised in Bangkok-Thonburi and Chiangmai, while one third of the doctors in Indonesia resided in Djakarta and a majority worked in large urban centres. These patterns are repeated almost everywhere in the region. Education and health are interrelated, since rural people cannot qualify for a professional medical education and doctors are not prepared to live outside the cities because of a dearth of good schools and other amenities for their families in the country.

Finally, the leadership of South-East Asia has actively and ardently set out to decrease the communal tensions that existed during the colonial and early nationalist years and to develop a sense of unity. This drive towards integration has been the core of the policies of the governing classes throughout the area as they seek to make nations out of the former colonies. To implement this process of unification they have employed a wide variety of techniques. Education has been the major tool, with concentrated efforts being made to instil national values into the young through texts, teaching and symbols. In Malaysia and Indonesia the national language has been utilized to bring together communal groups, though not without some foot-dragging from non-Malays in the former country. Ideology also has played a major part, particularly in Burma, Vietnam and Indonesia, and now in Malaysia, as leaders have extolled national values and traditions. Military training has helped to inculcate a sense of identity in the youth, who in turn have been sent out to the villages carrying the message of unity. Another factor, already noted, is seen in the programmes to expand communications through roads, air, radio, television, newspapers, etc. which have been inaugurated since the war. In most cases the central government maintains some control over the public dissemination of the spoken and written word, and a totally free Press is not to be found anywhere in the region (in Malaysia there is even a constitutional prohibition against attacking other races). National days bring together groups from throughout the country in an orgy of unity. Even clothing has been employed by the Burmese in an attempt to persuade tribal peoples to accept the ways of the majority by adopting the national costume. Other symbols are apparent to the traveller passing through rural areas as he sees pictures of Aung San in Burma, of the king in Thailand, of Sukarno previously and now Suharto in Indonesia and of the king and prime minister in Malaysia. All of this is to instil in the populace a sense of national unity, pride and purpose and to diminish the communal divisions that have been the despair of much of South-East Asia.

60 Unveiling of a statue of the martyred national hero Aung San in Rangoon, 1955 – part of the campaign to inculcate and strengthen national values.

As a result of these efforts, there have been noticeable examples of diminished communal tensions in the region. Christians in Indonesia have now largely been accepted into the political and bureaucratic system. This change was beginning to become apparent as early as the national and provincial elections in the 1950s, when Christian candidates were elected in constituencies with Moslem majorities. Christians have also served in cabinets through the years and provided essential members of the technocratic élite. There also appears to be less conflict than formerly between the Chinese and the Thais, although difficulties remain. The former have been willing to accept national customs, language and names, at least in part, and the Thai élite has worked out mutually advantageous accommodations with the Chinese business community. Boards of directors of Chinese companies often read like the *Who's Who* of the Thai bureaucratic and political élite, who provide protection in return for financial reimbursement. In spite of the communal riots of 1969, Malays and Chinese have lived together with less strain and considerably less violence than pessimists earlier predicted. While the riots revealed the severe fractures that still disturb national unity, they also impressed upon the respective communal élites the need for compromise.

It would be very misleading, however, to leave the impression that communal division does not continue to be a basic problem for most South-East Asian countries. In previous chapters we have commented upon the civil wars that have wracked the region. If in the more spectacular cases – the war in Indo-China and the anti-Communist purge in Indonesia – these are primarily ideological, there are others where the cause of conflict is communal friction. These include the lengthy civil war fought by the hill tribes in Burma, military actions against the Moros in the Philippines, the age-old antagonism between Vietnamese and Cambodians that has recently exploded into civilian massacres of both sides, and tribal and regional insurgence in north and north-east Thailand. These violent confrontations have usually taken place in outlying, sparsely populated areas and have caused fewer deaths than the ideological battles of Indo-China and Indonesia. However, they continue to necessitate heavy government expenditure on security, form obstacles to economic development, are used by the opposition to attack the national leadership and remain obvious symbols of disunity and unfinished nation-building.

In the urban centres, the position of the Chinese and Indians is still an unsolved problem, although in the past decades the governing classes have instituted a variety of policies to rid themselves of the issue. Throughout

123

most of South-East Asia, laws have been passed reserving specific professions or activities for the indigenous population or, as in Malaysia, establishing quotas limiting Chinese participation in education, the bureaucracy, the granting of licences, etc. In Indonesia and Burma these pariah communities have been forced out of their homes and businesses. Under Sukarno the Chinese were driven from towns and villages in the interior into hostile urban centres, causing many to return to China. The nationalization of commercial interests and the rapid growth of a virulent isolationist nationalism in Burma under the military resulted in the expulsion of tens of thousands of Indians. At a later stage the outbreak of riots (connected with the Great Proletarian Cultural Revolution in China) between young Chinese and Burmese in Rangoon and elsewhere resulted in sanctions against the Chinese community. However, governments have begun to discover that it is difficult to replace the loss of professional and commercial experience caused by the expulsion of these groups from the indigenous population, and a few leaders have belatedly begun to think about alternatives to such drastic action.

In sum, then, although difficulties remain, most of the major communal conflicts that spread across the region in the first two decades after the war have become more muted or have been relegated to the geographic fringes of the countries concerned. The development of communications, programmes of social welfare and sheer weariness of a constant state of war have led many to decide to make their peace with the government. The more pragmatic frame of reference of so much of the new leadership has also heightened the spirit of accommodation.

THE RISE OF THE 'NEW COLONIALISTS'

The changes that have taken place since independence may be regarded primarily as the result of technological modernization. In fact, the Westernized élites of the new states of South-East Asia have responded to developments which have touched every country in the world in the last generation. In no country has the leadership rejected Western standards of education and health and as a matter of fact they have improved substantially upon colonial practices. Nor have they turned their backs on the modern nation state as the vehicle of change. In the field of health the technicians dominate policy. In education it is much the same, although here governments have made major efforts to ensure that what is being learned is suited to what they regard as their own special needs. This has meant the increased use of national rather than European languages and the development of texts

61 Traditional mythology and national styles of art revived in a Thai children's book.

which discuss native problems and employ local illustrations. The day is past when Filipino children are taught about George Washington at Valley Forge or children in Indo-China or Malaysia are to memorize the names of French or English monarchs. In some cases, in Burma and Vietnam in particular, a number of programmes have been deliberately introduced to inculcate national ideologies into courses. Still, no controlling élite is demanding a return to teaching courses in Pali or Arabic and modern technological training is highly prized.

Some aspects of the legacy of the colonial past, on the other hand, have been counter-productive. The rural–urban gap was not invented by the European, but the inability to close it appreciably during his tenure of power has been a major obstacle to the expansion of educational and health opportunities. Furthermore, the aloof and often arrogant behaviour of the colonial civil servant has been inherited by the Asian bureaucrat. This, when combined with his attitudes of lack of interest or disdain towards traditionalist peasants, has made it difficult to integrate the rural and urban population and to facilitate development programmes in the countryside. One has only to observe a bureaucrat based in Bangkok, Djakarta or Saigon confronting a village meeting to understand the wide differences in attitudes, customs and values. In fact, it might almost be argued that one of the outstanding problems of modern South-East Asia is the emergence of what may be called the 'new colonialist'.

Indians like Nirad C. Chaudhuri have castigated the 'brown sahibs' who have muscled in as successors to the British, the local bosses of the Congress Party who ran the country after 1950. If in India there is a 'new Raj', in South-East Asia the 'new colonialists' are the successors to the colonial civil and military administrators and foreign capitalists of pre-independence days. The new élite is composed of Asian political leaders, upper-echelon bureaucrats, professionals and indigenous and Chinese entrepreneurs. In Burma the dominant members are the military, in Malaysia and Singapore the higher civil service, politicians and Chinese capitalists, while in most of the other countries a combination of all these interests is represented. We do not have sufficient insight into conditions in North Vietnam to know whether Milovan Djilas' 'new class' has taken over in that Communist country also.

The power and status of the 'new colonialists' rest essentially on the same foundations as did those of the old colonial élite – namely, wealth, education and access to the apparatus of modern industrial society. The years since independence have provided a multitude of new economic opportunities to gain security and wealth. Success has been achieved by men who took advantage of the withdrawal of European and non-indigenous Asian commercial interests, had access to sources of information revealing special opportunities, or, all too often, who did not shrink from corruption. It has also resulted from co-operation between those in political power and local and foreign capitalists. Not, of course, that corruption is the only road to wealth and advancement. On the contrary, efforts to foster local talent so as to provide a replacement for non-nationals and the sheer speed of modernization opened glittering prospects for bright young bureaucrats and businessmen. It must also be said that not all the ruling classes of South-East Asia have succumbed in the same way to the temptation of economic self-aggrandizement. This is true both of the Burmese military and of the Vietnamese Communists. However, with the exceptions of North Vietnam and Burma, there has been no significant redistribution of income in the area and the 'new colonialists' are members of a very small minority at the highest income levels.

We have noted that modern university and technical education is primarily the prerogative of the urban economic and political élite. The result has been the development of a self-perpetuating group whose power is based upon technical and administrative superiority over the rural peasantry and urban workers, in much the same way as the European colonial administrations maintained their superiority over their Asian subjects after the Industrial Revolution. This situation was made permanent through the availability of scholarships to prestigious institutions of higher learning for those with political contacts. Furthermore, wealthy indigenous and Chinese parents were able to place their children in overseas institutions when they were unable to qualify for the better national universities. Although the pattern is changing, the paucity of decent primary and secondary schools in the rural areas, combined with the prestige of some universities with limited enrolments, will perpetuate these conditions for many years to come.

Residence in urban areas, particularly in the capital cities, affords the 'new colonialists' advantages not available to their rural countrymen. It is in the capital that the élite finds high-quality medical facilities, cultural opportunities such as theatres, cinemas and television, the cultural amenities associated with universities, the chance to interact with the foreign community and learn about new techniques developed abroad, and an intellectual and political life that is rarely evident in rural areas. The life style of the new élite is also entirely different from that of the villager or provincial

62–65 The gulf between the developing urban centres and the backward rural population persists almost everywhere in the region, and seems likely to become a major problem. Below, change is coming slowly to the countryside: traditional ploughing in Thailand and (above right) Vietnamese peasants working in the paddyfields. Above, typical weekday traffic in sophisticated Bangkok, and (below right) urban construction workers in Manila.

66 A symbol of the future or remembrance of times past? A child plays with artillery rounds near Danang, South Vietnam.

townsman. He has electricity, good restaurants and hotels, new auto-mobiles, Western-type housing, air-conditioning and other benefits of a modern urban environment. Here again, the disparities are similar to those between the European colonial élite and South-East Asians in the pre-war period.

Finally, the attitudes of the 'new colonialists' towards country people and provincials are all too often a contemporary reproduction of the contemptuous attitude that Europeans had towards their Asian subjects. The peasants are characterized as ignorant, superstitious, uneducable, and without ideas. Bureaucrats scheme to occupy positions in the capital and escape provincial posts, and the urban élite is often completely ignorant of national life outside a few cities. It is a paradox that South-East Asia in the past two decades has developed a new élite with all the essential characteristics of the agents of European imperialism against whom the nationalists struggled for so many years. It is also a dangerous omen for the future.

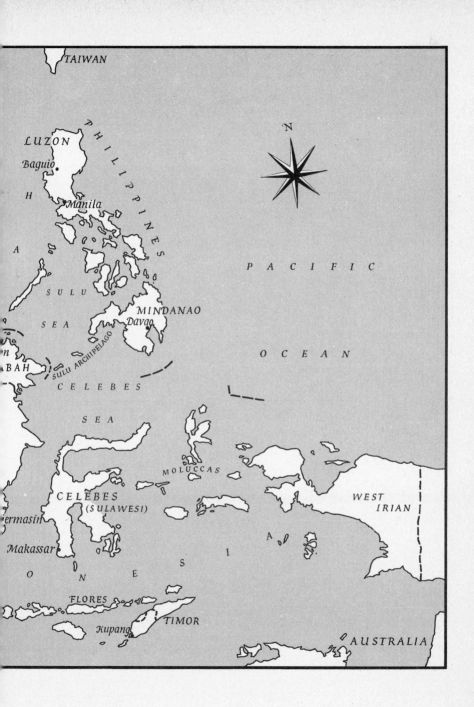

Chronology

COLONIAL PERIOD

1885 British complete annexation of Burma
1887 French form Indo-China of Vietnam and Cambodia
1893 French established protectorate over Laos
1895 Malay Federation formed
1898 Aguinaldo declares abortive Philippine independence
Spain cedes the Philippines to the United States
1901 Dutch promulgate Ethical Policy
1918 Volksraad formed in the Dutch East Indies
1926–27 Abortive Communist-led rebellion in the Dutch East Indies
1930 'Red Terror' in Indo-China followed by the 'White Terror'
1932 Coup ends the absolute monarchy in Thailand
1934 Tydings-McDuffie Act promises independence to the Philippines in
1946
1935 Burma separated from India
1937 Constitution established in Burma

SECOND WORLD WAR PERIOD

1941 Sihanouk becomes king of Cambodia at 18
Formation of the Viet Minh by Ho Chi Minh
Establishment of the Burmese Independence Army by Aung San
Japanese attack Pearl Harbor and South-East Asia
1942 Thailand declares war on the United Kingdom and the United States
Japan occupies Burma, Malaya, the Philippines and the Dutch East
Indies
Sihanouk declares Cambodian independence under Japanese guidance
1943 Indonesia takes first steps toward independence under the Japanese
Ba Maw declares Burmese independence under the Japanese

Laurel declares Philippine independence under the Japanese
Burma declares war on the Allies
1945 Japan ends French rule in Indo-China
Emperor Bao Dai declares Vietnamese independence
Japan surrenders
Sukarno and Hatta declare Indonesian independence

POST-WAR INDEPENDENCE AND NATIONALIST PERIOD

1946 Philippine independence established
French and Viet Minh begin major hostilities
1947 Aung San assassinated
Malay Federation re-established
Dutch launch first 'police action' against the Indonesian Republic
1948 Burmese independence established outside the Commonwealth
Communist rebellions begin in Burma, the Philippines, Malaya and
Indonesia
Laos declared independent under French protection
Dutch launch second 'police action', capturing most Republican
leaders
1949 Round Table Conference ends Indonesian–Dutch struggle
1954 Fall of Dien Bien Phu
Geneva Conference divides Vietnam and provides full independence
for Laos and Cambodia
SEATO formed
1957 Malayan independence established
1958 Rebellion on Indonesian outer islands
Coup in Burma brings Ne Win to power
1959 Sukarno re-establishes 1945 Constitution
Singapore granted independence within Commonwealth
1960 Elections in Burma bring the return of U Nu
1962 Coup returns Ne Win to power
1963 Ngo Dinh Diem assassinated, end of civilian rule in South Vietnam
Malaysia formed, including Singapore
1965 Singapore leaves Malaysia
Attempted coup in Indonesia leads to rule by military and downfall of
Sukarno and the PKI

American military involvement in Vietnam widens
1968 Talks begin in Paris to end the war in Indo-China
Suharto becomes President of Indonesia
1969 Constitutional rule re-established in Thailand
Communal riots bring temporary suspension of Malaysian Parliament
1970 Sihanouk deposed
1971 Military topples constitutional government in Thailand
1972 Marcos ends political system established at Philippine independence
1973 Peace agreement completed on Vietnam War
American troops leave Indo-China
Coalition established between Lao Government and Pathet Lao
Student-led uprising topples Thai military government

Notes and Bibliography

CHAPTER 1

1 The following information is primarily drawn from von der Mehden, Fred R., *Religion and Nationalism in Southeast Asia*, Madison, Wis., 1963.
2 See Furnivall, J.S., *Colonial Policy and Practice*, Cambridge, 1948.
3 Hammer, Ellen, *The Struggle for Indo-China*, Stanford, Calif., 1954, 79.
4 Orwell, George, *Burmese Days*, New York, 1934, London, 1935.
5 Sjarhir, S., *Out of Exile*, New York, 1949.

CHAPTER 2

1 For the background to this period see Toland, J., *The Rising Sun*, New York, 1970; Benda, H., *The Crescent and the Rising Sun: Indonesian Islam under the Japanese Occupation, 1942–1945*, The Hague, 1958; Elsbree, W., *Japan's Role in Southeast Asian Nationalist Movements, 1940 to 1945*, Cambridge, Mass., 1953.
2 Dr Ba Maw's position in those years is described in his *Breakthrough in Burma*, New Haven, Conn., and London, 1968.

CHAPTER 3

1 Facts on rehabilitation are drawn from Paauw, D., 'Economic Progress in Southeast Asia', *Journal of Asian Studies*, November, 1963, 69–72.
2 For a compendium of Sukarno's major early speeches see *Towards Freedom and the Dignity of Man*, Djakarta, n.d.
3 Quoted in Butwell, R., *U Nu of Burma*, Stanford, Calif., 1969.

CHAPTER 4

1 U Nu, 'Asians and Democracy', *Burma Weekly Bulletin*, 24 November 1960, 287, 291.
2 For a discussion of Sihanouk's position see Armstrong, J., *Sihanouk Speaks*, New York, 1964.
3 Sukarno, op. cit., 14.
4 Ibid., 142.
5 Quoted in Walinsky, L.J., *Economic Development in Burma, 1951–1960*, New York, 1962, 63.

6 Butwell, op. cit., 74.
7 Quoted in Gettleman, M., ed., *Vietnam*, Greenwich, Conn., 1965, Harmondsworth, 1966, 33.
8 Sukarno, op. cit., 14.
9 See von der Mehden, Fred R., 'The Burmese Way to Socialism', *Asian Survey*, March 1963, 129–35.
10 Quoted in Hindley, D., 'Indonesia 1971: Pantja Sila Democracy and the Second Parliamentary Elections', *Asian Survey*, January 1972, 58.
11 See Mya Maung, 'The Burmese Way to Socialism Beyond the Welfare State', *Asian Survey*, June 1970, 533–51.
12 *The Burmese Way to Socialism*, Rangoon, n.d.
13 Sukarno, op. cit., 65.
14 *Siam Rath*, 26 December 1967.
15 Sukarno, op. cit., 75.
16 *Malay Mail*, 29 August 1970.
17 Quoted in Milne, R.S., '"National Ideology" and Nation-Building in Malaysia', *Asian Survey*, July 1970, 566.

CHAPTER 5

There are few good descriptions or analytical surveys of institutions in contemporary South-East Asia. Some of the better studies of particular countries are Feith, Herbert, *The Decline of Constitutional Democracy in Indonesia*, Ithaca, N.Y., 1962; Wilson, D., *Politics in Thailand*, Ithaca, N.Y., 1962; Fall, B., *The Two Viet-nams*, London and New York, 1963; Means, G., *Malaysian Politics*, London and New York, 1970; Milne, R.S., *Government and Politics in Malaysia*, Boston, 1967; Tinker, H., *Union of Burma*, London, 1957; Hayden, J., *The Philippines*, New York, 1942. For studies of the military see *Is Trust Vindicated?*, Rangoon, 1960; Roeder, O., *The Smiling General: President Soeharto of Indonesia*, Djakarta, 1970; and the November 1970 issue of *Journal of Comparative Administration*, which deals with the military in Asia.

CHAPTER 6

Statistics for this chapter were drawn primarily from United Nations data.

137

List of Illustrations

21 Surrender of Singapore, 15 February 1942. Photo: Imperial War Museum.

22 The cookhouse, Changi gaol, Singapore; painting by Leslie Cole. Photo: Camera Press.

23 President Sukarno at reception at Merdeka Palace, 1967. Photo: Camera Press (Bill Lord).

24 Men of a Sikh regiment fighting in Burma, 1945. Photo: Imperial War Museum.

25 The Japanese Octopus; poster by Pat Keely, published for the Dutch Government in Exile, 1944. Photo: Imperial War Museum.

26 President Manuel L. Quezon of the Philippines, taking the oath, 1935; detail of mural by Carlos V. Francisca in Manila City Hall.

27 Filipino patriot reports to United States Army. Photo: Imperial War Museum.

28 Aung San, in London, 1947. Photo: Radio Times Hulton Picture Library.

29 General William C. Westmoreland and Air Vice-Marshal Nguyen cao Ky taking the salute in South Vietnam, 1968. Photo: Courtesy Vietnam Embassy, London.

30 Government troops and civilians, Burma, 1949. Photo: Radio Times Hulton Picture Library.

31 Burmese naval patrol on the Irrawaddy, 1949. Photo: Radio Times Hulton Picture Library.

32 South Vietnamese soldier. Photo: Courtesy Vietnam Embassy, London.

33 Thai Buddhist monk. Photo: M. Hürlimann.

34 Parliament House, Kuala Lumpur. Photo: Courtesy Malaysian Information Services.

35 Election poster, Singapore, 1955. Photo: Courtesy Malaysian Information Services.

36 President Suharto addressing People's Congress. Photo: Courtesy Indonesian Embassy, London.

37 Ho Chi Minh; North Vietnamese poster.

38 North Vietnamese children taking shelter. Photo: Novosti.

39 American soldier fighting in Vietnam; Cuban poster.

40 Nationalized brewery and distillery, Mandalay, Burma. Photo: Associated Press.

41 Supermarket, Kuala Lumpur, Malaysia, 1972. Photo: Courtesy Metal Box Company.

42 Street on Basilan Island in the Philippines. Photo: Camera Press (J. Ph. Charbonnier).

43 Anniversary of independence celebration, at Phnom Penh, capital of Cambodia, 1955. Photo: Keystone Press Agency.

44 King Bhumibol Adulyadej of Thailand. Photo: Courtesy Thai Embassy, London.

45 Indonesian election posters, 1955. Photo: Camera Press.

46 Elections in South Vietnam; cartoon from *Krokodil*, 1967. School of Slavonic Studies, University of London.

47 The President of the Malaysian Senate, Dato Haji Abdul Rahman bin Mohd Yasin (left), talking to the Speaker of the Lower House, Tuan Haji Mohd Noah bin Omar. Photo: Courtesy Malaysian Information Services.

48 President Suharto of Indonesia receiving a rifle from the visiting French Chief of Staff, Marshal Michel Forguet. Photo: Camera Press.

49 General Ne Win of Burma. Photo: Keystone Press Agency.

50 Prince Norodom Sihanouk of Cambodia addressing a meeting in Peking, May 1970.

51 Tengku Abdul Rahman opening Esso Oil refinery, Port Dickson, 1964. Photo: Courtesy Malaysian Information Services.

52 U Nu giving funds for the Sixth Buddhist Synod; cartoon from *The Guardian*, Rangoon, 1956.

53 Asia Insurance building, Singapore. Photo: Camera Press.

54 Girls' High School, Saigon, 1970. Photo: Courtesy Vietnam Embassy, London.

55 Kindergarten in Thailand. Photo: Camera Press.

56 Vice-Chancellor of the University of Singapore making a speech on Graduation Day.

57 Literary class in Malaya, 1954. Courtesy Unesco.

58 Biology class at Hué University Medical School. Photo: Courtesy Vietnam Embassy, London.

59 Vaccination in rural Malaysia. Photo: Courtesy Malaysian Information Services, London.

60 Unveiling of statue of Aung San, Rangoon, 1955. Photo: Associated Press.

61 Illustration from book of Thai folk-tales, published Bangkok, 1963.

62 Ploughing in Thailand. Photo: Courtesy Thai Embassy, London.

63 Vietnamese peasants working in paddy-fields. Photo: Courtesy Vietnam Embassy, London.

64 Traffic in Bangkok. Photo: Courtesy Thai Embassy, London.

65 Construction workers in Manila. Photo: Camera Press.

66 Child playing with artillery rounds, South Vietnam, 1973. Photo: Associated Press.

Index

Page numbers in italics refer to illustrations

Kachins 48, 62, 92
Karens 37, 48, 62, 64, 65, 92
Ky, Nguyen cao 58

Lamitan 90
language 28, 121, 126
Laurel, José 46
Lee Kuan Yew 86, 110, 111, 112
legislature: 24, 98–103; Burma 98–100;
 Indo-China 26, 98–100; Indonesia 25,
 98–102; Malaysia 99–103; Philippines
 98, 99; Singapore 103; Thailand 99,
 102
Lenin, Nicolai 20, 37
Lincoln, Abraham 71, 75
Lon Nol, General 80, 81, 100, 106

MacArthur, General Douglas 42, 51
Mahjapahit empire 21
Malayan Communist Party 92, 114
Malayan People's Anti-Japanese Army
 59
Malaysia: colonial system 22; consti-
 tution 71, 108–14, 122; democracy 76,
 77, 82; education 117, 118; executive
 98; health 120; independence 75;
 Japanese occupation 12, 41, 59, 109;
 legislature 99–103; nationalism 59
Marcos, Ferdinand 78, 80–81, 106
Marx, Karl 20
Marxism 36, 37, 54, 65, 73, 74, 75, 78, 79,
 82–83, 86
Mazzini, Giuseppe 38, 75
Merdeka (Indonesian independence) 75
Ministry of National Unity (Malaysia)
 94
missionaries 19, 20, 31, 64
Molière, Jean-Baptiste 20
Moros 92, 123
Moslems see Islam
mufukat (Indonesian political principle)
 73

musjarawah (Indonesian political principle) 73

National Assembly (South Vietnam) 100
National Executive Council (Thailand)
 100
nationalism: 31, 34, 36–37, 46–48, 51–68,
 75–76, 88–93; Burma 30, 40, 51–54,
 88; Indo-China 26–27, 53–60; Indonesia 25, 35–37, 53–59, 66, 88; Malaysia 59; Philippines 23, 51, 66–67;
 Thailand 30, 88–91
'new colonialists' 124–31
Ne Win, General 41, 78, 88, 105, 107, 111
Ngo Dinh Diem 45, 66, 76, 82, 88, 94,
 95, 98, 105, 111
Nkrumah, Kwame 66
Nu, U 20, 37, 39, 45, 65, 70–71, 73–74,
 75, 76, 86, 95, 98, 110, 111, 111

Ortega y Gasset, José 38
Orwell, George 27
OSS (Office of Strategic Services) 50
Ottuma, U 31

Pali 18, 126
Pantja Sila 73, 74, 75–76, 80
Pantja Sila Democracy 81, 100
Partai Kommunist Indonesia (PKI) 25,
 36, 74, 92
Pearl Harbor 42
People's Action Party (Malaysia) 112
People's Congress (Indonesia) 81
People's Stores (Burma) 86
permusjarawatan (Indonesian political
 principle) 73
personalism (Ngo Dinh Diem) 94
perwakilan (Indonesian political prin-
 ciple) 73
Pétain régime 42
Philippines: colonial system 66–67;
 constitution 108; coup, 1972: 100,